TRADITIONAL
KNITTING
FOR CHILDREN
AND BEARS

TRADITIONAL KNITTING FOR CHILDREN AND BEARS

Furze Hewitt

Photography by Robert Roach
Line illustrations by Josephine Hoggan

Kangaroo Press

To Simon, Alice, Angus, Robert, William and James

Acknowledgments

This book would not have been possible without the expertise of the following people:

- Robert Roach, photographer, for his skill in photographing the knitting.
- Josephine Hoggan, artist, for her charming drawings.
- Dina Tagliapietra for typing the manuscript.
- The knitters: Edna Lomas, Joan Eckersley, Eileen Kerney, Ruth Tyrie, Ruth Rintoule, Barbara Hosking, Betty Featherstone, Dulcie Brewer, Thea Moore, Kathy Grin.
- The embroiderers: Kathie Savage, Joan Jackson.
- The models: Alice, Annalise, Annika, Jessica.
- Carol Davey, Patricia Wain, Patricia Blyth, Pat Walsh, Danny McCheane, Douglas Wilson for providing articles to use in the sets.
- John Cummins of Queanbeyan Books and Prints for locating old knitting publications.
- Esther and Jeannette from Evergreen Florist, Manuka ACT for supplying silk flowers.
- Effie Mitrofanis and DMC Needlecraft Pty Ltd for their interest and generous support in supplying the DMC cottons used in producing the book.
- My appreciation to the following for their help in various ways: Robert Colquhoun, Alice Cottee, Roslyn Panetta, Carol Coates, Isabel Bunting, Rita Horn, Anne Savage, Michael Roath, Maurine Rogers, Keith Hewitt, Patsy Ranger, Anna Sliwinski, Rina Tagliapietra, James Botham, Susie Wilson, Henry and Jacqi Koselski, Maree Lever.

Technical note

All the photographs in this book were taken using:

- Kodak Ektachrome Plus, Professional, 35 mm daylight slide film, processed by Kodak.
- Zeiss Ikon/Voigtländer Icarex 35S camera with Carl Zeiss Ultron 50 mm Fl 8 lens (bought in 1970).

First published in 1995 by Kangaroo Press Pty Ltd
3 Whitehall Road Kenthurst NSW 2156 Australia
PO Box 6125 Dural Delivery Centre NSW 2158 Australia
Typeset by in Australia by Lynwood Press, Kulnura 2250
Printed in China through Global-Com Pte Ltd

ISBN 0 86417 687 2

Contents

A selection of white knitted articles from this book.

Introduction

This book is the result of collecting and preserving old knitting patterns over several decades.

I share my interest in preserving old patterns with the knitters listed in the acknowledgments. Each knitter has a preferred medium. Eileen Kerney knits children's garments in wool. Edna Lomas' preference is for dainty lace gowns, Ruth Rintoule's for fine even work in cotton as seen in the christening gown.

Barbara Hosking is keen to preserve *anything* to do with knitting; she delighted in preserving the Bendigo Shawl design. This pattern is one I received from Zimbabwe, the design dating from the turn of the century. Barbara also deciphered the instructions used by Ruth Rintoule, Betty Featherstone and Dulcie Brewer, notably the Victorian Collar dated 1897 which needed to be carefully dissected, an extremely laborious task. Thanks to Barbara, the collar has been knitted by Dulcie and preserved for future knitters to enthuse over.

Ruth Tyrie made the Snowflakes cot cover, a beautiful piece of knitting in a heavier yarn for warmth and ease of laundering. Joan Eckersley is a perfectionist, whatever the medium—her coathangers and towels are exquisite. Ruth Rintoule and Dulcie Brewer combined their skills in knitting the one-ply shawl. Thea Moore knitted Theodore. The bear is part of the extensive David Moore collection. Kathy Grin made Burnous, the cape and hood worn by Annalise and knitted in 2-ply wool. Betty Featherstone made the unusual hot water bottle cover and sachet. All of these items have been adapted from old patterns for this book.

My own preference is for fine knitting, as shown on the Talisman christening robe. The lace complements Kathie Savage's skill as a needleworker.

Joan Jackson is another needleworker of exceptional skill. We are fortunate to include her work demonstrating the restrained use of embroidery to enhance white cotton knitting.

Josephine Hoggan, in her inimitable style, has created drawings appropriate for the theme of the book, while the Robert Roach studies of the children wearing the garments capture the timeless charm of the designs.

The book should offer enticements to all knitters, and inspire those of moderate skills to attempt some of the designs.

Happy knitting.

Furze Hewitt, 1995

Abbreviations and Terms

Abbreviations are used in knitting instructions to save space, and to make the patttern easier to follow. It is important to read, and understand, the abbreviations before beginning to knit a pattern.

In this book most of the patterns use standard British abbreviations.

In ordinary knitting the made sts consist of the following:

yfwd	between two knit stitches
yon	between a purl and knit action
yrn	between two purl actions

In this book the above actions are referred to as m1 — make one, as they are commonly written in old lace patterns.

Some helpful abbreviations

k	knit
p	purl
st	stitch
sts	stitches
b	back
f	front
sl	slip
wyib	with yarn in back
wyif	with yarn in front
tog	together
*m1	make one stitch by winding yarn round needle
turn	work is turned before end of row
dpn	double pointed needle
motif	design unit
st, st	stocking stitch — knit right side, purl wrong side
garter st	knit all rows
mb	make bobble
beg	beginning
psso	pass slipped stitch over
p2sso	pass 2 slipped stitches over
p-wise	purlwise
k-wise	knitwise

*In old knitting publications the increase in lace knitting was referred to in several different ways: o — over; m1 — make one; and cast up.

tbl	through back of loop
ybk	yarn back
yfwd	yarn forward
yon	yarn over needle
yrn	yarn around needle
R.H.	right hand
L.H.	left hand
tw st	twist stitch
inc	increase
dc	double crochet
ch	chain

Comparative terms

British	American
cast off	bind off
tension	gauge
alternate rows	every other row
miss	skip
work straight	work even
stocking stitch	stockinette stitch
shape cap	shape top

Knitting needle sizes

Metric	British	American
2 mm	14	00
2.25	13	0
2.75	12	1
3	11	2
3.25	10	3
3.75	9	4
4	8	5
4.5	7	6
5	6	7
5.5	5	8
6	4	9
6.5	3	10
7	2	10½
7.5	1	11
8	0	12
9	00	13
10	000	15

Techniques

Casting on

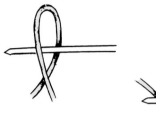

Step 1

Step 2

Step 3

Step 4

Thumb method of casting on

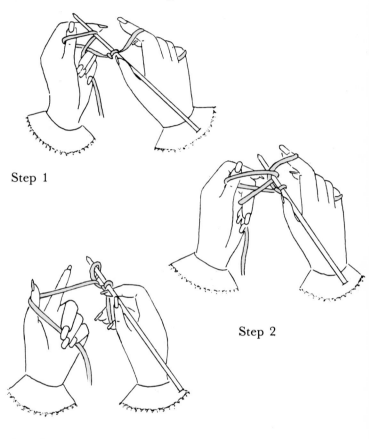

Step 1

Step 2

Step 3

How to knit

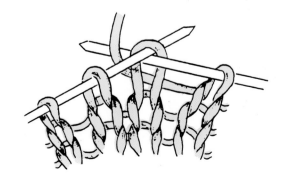

How to purl

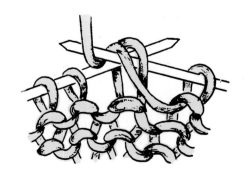

Invisible cast on method

1. Using contrasting thread, cast on the number of stitches required, work two rows in stocking stitch.
2. With main thread, continue work until length required.
3. When work is completed, remove contrasting thread. Either graft or sew together open stitches from both ends of work.

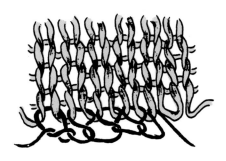

Increasing in lace knitting

There are three methods of increasing the number of stitches on a row, or in a round. One way is to knit twice into a stitch (Fig. 1). This increase can be worked k-wise or p-wise. Read your pattern carefully and work as directed.

A second method is to pick up a loop between two sts, and knit into that loop (Fig. 2). This prevents a hole forming in the knitting.

The third method (Fig. 3), make one (or m1), produces the holes in lace knitting. The way it is worked depends on whether the extra stitch is to be made between two knit stitches, a knit and a purl, or two purl stitches. Between knit sts the yarn is brought forward, and over the needle as you knit the next stitch, thus forming a new stitch. Once again, read your pattern carefully.

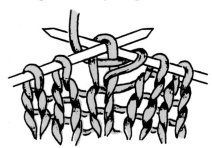

Fig. 1

Fig. 2

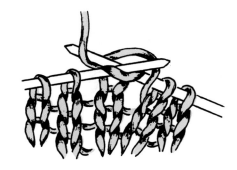

Fig. 3

(a) Make one between two knit stitches

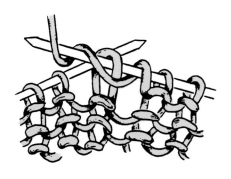

(b) Make one between two purl stitches

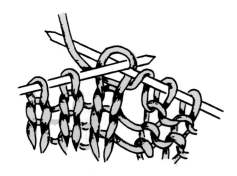

(c) Make one between a knit and a purl stitch

Decreasing in lace knitting

Again there are several methods. One method is to knit or purl two stitches together (Fig. 4a and b). A second method is to pass the second last stitch previously worked over the last one (Fig. 4c and d).

Fig. 4 (a)

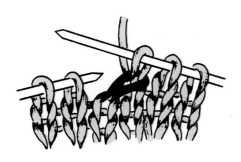

(b)

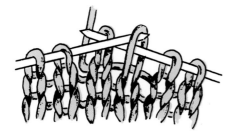

(c)

(d)

Knitted picot cast off

Knit 1st st. *Sl 1 st from R.H. needle on to L.H. needle. Insert needle into this st, cast on 2 sts, then cast off 5 sts. Repeat from * until all sts have been cast off.

Knitting off your stitches if you can't crochet

K1, *k2 tog, m1, k2 tog, turn. P1, [(k1, p1) twice, k1] in next stitch.
P1, sl 1 purlwise, turn. Cast off 7 sts (1 st left on R.H. needle)*.
Repeat from *–* to last 5 sts. K3 tog, m1, k2 tog, turn, p1, (k1, p1) twice, k1, in next st, p1, sl 1 purlwise, turn. Cast off remaining sts.
For a larger loop on your edging, make 9 sts instead of the 5 sts described above.

Grafting

A simplified method from Barbara Hosking
Place two needles, each with equal number of sts, wrong sides together.
   Thread bodkin with matching yarn. Insert bodkin knitwise into first st on front needle, slip off. Insert bodkin into second st purlwise, leave on needle. Insert bodkin through first st on back needle purlwise, slip off. Thread through second st knitwise, leave on needle. Repeat thus until grafting is completed.

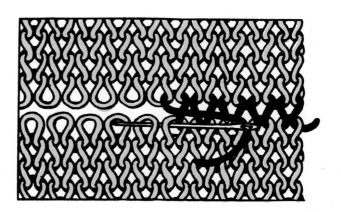

Tension

Experienced knitters know if their tension varies from the average. Early knitting instructions seldom have tensions given. The chart below is a basic guide to assist knitters of average tension.

Basic tension table gives average tension in st, st over 2.5 cm (1″)

Needle Size	2-ply	3-ply	4-ply
12	9 sts	8½ sts	8 sts
11	8½ sts	8 sts	7½ sts
10	8 sts	7½ sts	7 sts
9	7½ sts	7 sts	6½ sts
8	7 sts	6½ sts	6 sts
7	6½ sts	6 sts	5½ sts

Lace knitters rely on their choice of yarn and needles and on the weight of the article being knitted, and adjust their knitting materials accordingly.

Suggested needles and cotton

Tray cloths, table cloths, small items of napery: Needles 2 mm (14), cotton 20
Lingerie: Needles 1.75 mm (15), cotton 30–40
Infants' wear, lawn, linen, liberty cottons: Needles 1.25 mm (18), cottons 80–100
Handkerchiefs, fine voiles and baptistes: Needles 1.00 mm (20), cottons 80–100

Tension in the knitter

Knitting is for pleasure; to help you enjoy your chosen craft I suggest a few simple actions to relieve tension in your hands, wrists and neck.

Using unaccustomed needles and yarns can cause stiffness in the hands, so try some imaginary piano playing on a firm surface, then stretch the fingers slowly, spreading them as far as you possibly can, then relax them.

Keep a discarded ball of yarn to exercise your hands. Place ball in the palm and stretch your fingers around it, then relax whole hand. Do this several times then repeat in other hand.

Make sure your hands are smooth and your needles in good condition. These are your most important tools and need your care. Hands can benefit from an application of exfoliating scrub, followed by a nourishing hand lotion.

Stiff neck and shoulders will ease if you adjust your posture. Sit up in your chair. To relax the tension in your neck and shoulders, let your shoulders relax and your head drop forward. Do this a few times during a long knitting session. Your eyes can cause tension too. Make sure you have a good light source.

Enjoy your knitting.

THE PATTERNS

1: RUTH EVELYN

This special occasion outfit suitable for a christening was designed and made by Ruth Rintoule of Lalor, Victoria. The lace panelled gown has matching bonnet and bootees. Ruth has included a dainty pillowcase and lace trimmed handkerchief with these patterns. Ruth Evelyn is modelled by three months old Annalise O'Toole.

Materials

Gown and bonnet: 25 × 20 g balls of DMC 20 cotton (Blanc) 5200; needles 2 mm (14) and set of 2 mm (14) for bonnet
Pillowcase: 2 × 20 g balls of DMC 20 cotton (Blanc) 5200; needles size 2 mm (14)
Handkerchief: 1 ball DMC 100 cotton (Blanc); needles size 1.25 mm (18)
Ribbons: 1 m (1 yd) for bonnet, 4 m (4¾ yds) narrow ribbon for gown (width and texture of ribbon your choice)
Skein of DMC stranded cotton
Small pillowcase
Plain white hemstitched linen handkerchief
Fine cotton thread for sewing
4 small flat white buttons

Measurements

Underarm 31 cm (12¼")
Neck to hem 63.5 cm (25")
Sleeves 5 cm (2")
Skirt width 129 cm (51")
Tension: 13 sts to 2.5 cm (1") over st, st

CHRISTENING GOWN

Front panel of skirt

Cast on 70 sts.
Work 10 cm (4") st, st.

Next row: Continue in st, st, * k2 tog each end of the needle.
Work another 10 cm (4″) *. Repeat *–* until panel measures 42 cm (16½″) (244 rows).
Cast off.

Side panels of skirt (make 2)

Cast on 170 sts.
Work 230 rows st, st.
Row 231: K80. Cast off 10 sts. K to end of row
Row 232: ** Purl.
Row 233: K2 tog. K to last 2 sts, k2 tog **.
Repeat **–** 4 times.
Row 243: Purl.
Row 244: (K3 tog) to end of row.
Row 245: Purl.
Cast off.

Back panel of skirt

Cast on 70 sts.
Work as front panel until row 210.
Row 211: K32. Turn (leaving remaining sts on needle), cast on 4 sts and work to correspond with other side.
Cast off.

Shoulder pieces (make 2)

Cast on 30 sts.
Work 7 rows st, st. Continue in st, st.
Row 8: Inc each end of row.
Next row: As row 8 until shoulder piece measures 8 cm (3¼″) 42 sts.
Cast off.

Sleeves (make 2)

Cast on 108 sts. Work 4 rows st, st.
Row 5: (K2, k2 tog) to end of row.
Row 6: Purl.
Row 7: Knit.
Row 8: Purl.
Row 9: K1, k2 tog, (m2, k2, k2 tog) to the last 2 sts, m2, k2.
Row 10: Purl (dropping 1 loop of the m2 of previous row).
Row 11: Knit.
Row 12: Purl.
Row 13: K2, inc in each st, until last 2 sts, k2.
Work 5 rows, st, st.
Rows 19 and 20: Cast off 5 sts at beginning of row. Work k2 tog at both ends of alternate rows until 40 sts remain.
Next row: K1, (k2 tog) to end of row. Cast off purlwise.

BERRY AND LEAF LACE

Cast on 39 sts.
Row 1: K2, m1, p2 tog, k2, m1, k4, k2 tog, p1, k2 tog, k4, m1, p1, m1, k4, k2 tog, p1, k2 tog, k4, m1, k2, m1, p2 tog, k2.
Row 2: K2, m1, p2 tog, k2, p6, (k1, p6) 3 times, k2, m1, p2 tog, k2.
Row 3: K2, m1, p2 tog, k2, m1, k4, k2 tog, p1, k2 tog, k4, m1, p1, m1, k4, k2 tog, p1, k2 tog, k4, m1, k2, m1, p2 tog, k2.
Row 4: As row 2.
Row 5: K2, m1, p2 tog, k2, m1, k2 tog, k2, k2 tog, p1, k2 tog, k2, k2 tog, m1, p1, m1, k2 tog, k2, k2 tog, p1, k2 tog, k2, k2 tog, m1, k2, m1, p2 tog, k2.
Row 6: K2, m1, p2 tog, k2, p5, (k1, p5) 3 times, k2, m1, p2 tog, k2.
Row 7: K2, m1, p2 tog, k2, m1, k1, m1, k4, p1, k3, k2 tog, m1, p1, m1, k2 tog, k3, p1, k4, m1, k1, m1, k2, m1, p2 tog, k2.
Row 8: K2, m1, p2 tog, k2, p7, (k1, p5) twice, k1, p7, k2, m1, p2 tog, k2.
Row 9: K2, m1, p2 tog, k2, m1, k3, m1, k2, k2 tog, p1, k2 tog, k3, p1, k3, k2 tog, p1, k2 tog, k2, m1, k3, m1, k2, m1, p2 tog, k2.
Row 10: K2, m1, p2 tog, k2, p8, (k1, p4) twice, k1, p8, k2, m1, p2 tog, k2.
Row 11: K2, m1, p2 tog, k2, m1, k5, m1, k1, k2 tog, p1, (k2 tog) twice, p1, (k2 tog) twice, p1, k2 tog, k1, m1, k5, m1, k2, m1, p2 tog, k2.
Row 12: K2, m1, p2 tog, k2, p9, (k1, p2) twice, k1, p9, k2, m1, p2 tog, k2.
Row 13: K2, m1, p2 tog, k2, m1, k3, p1, k3, m1, k2 tog, (p1, k2 tog) 3 times, m1, k3, p1, k3, m1, k2, m1, p2 tog, k2.
Row 14: K2, m1, p2 tog, k2, p4, k1, p5, (k1, p1) twice, k1, p5, k1, p4, k2, m1, p2 tog, k2.
Row 15: K2, m1, p2 tog, k2, m1, k4, p1, k4, m1, k3 tog, p1, k3 tog, m1, k4, p1, k4, m1, k2, m1, p2 tog, k2.
Row 16: K2, m1, p2 tog, k2, p5, (k1, p6) twice, k1, p5, k2, m1, p2 tog, k2.
Row 17: K2, m1, p2 tog, k2, m1, k5, p1, k5, m1, k3 tog, m1, k5, p1, k5, m1, k2, m1, p2 tog, k2.
Row 18: K2, m1, p2 tog, k2, p6, k1, p13, k1, p6, k2, m1, p2 tog, k2.
Row 19: K2, m1, p2 tog, k2, m1, k4, k2 tog, p1, k2 tog, k4, m1, p1, m1, k4, k2 tog, p1, k2 tog, k4, m1, k2, m1, p2 tog, k2.
Row 20: As row 2.
Row 21: As row 1.
Row 22: As row 2.
Row 23: As row 1.
Row 24: As row 2.
Row 25: As row 1.
Row 26: As row 2.

Row 27: K2, m1, p2 tog, k2, m1, k2 tog, k2, k2 tog, p1, k2 tog, k2, k2 tog, m1, p1, m1, k2 tog, k2, k2 tog, p1, k2 tog, k2, k2 tog, m1, k2, m1, p2 tog, k2.

Row 28: K2, m1, p2 tog, k2, p5, (k1, p5) 3 times, k2, m1, p2 tog, k2.

Row 29: K2, m1, p2 tog, k2, m1, (k1, p1 in next st) m1, k4, p1, k3, k2 tog, m1, p1, m1, k2 tog, k3, p1, k4, m1, (k1, p1 in next st) m1, k2, m1, p2 tog, k2.

Row 30: K2, m1, p2 tog, k6, p4, (k1, p5) twice, k1, p4, k6, m1, p2 tog, k2.

Row 31: K2, m1, p2 tog, k2, m1, p4, m1, k2, k2 tog, p1, k2 tog, k3, p1, k3, k2 tog, p1, k2 tog, k2, m1, p4, m1, k2, m1, p2 tog, k2.

Row 32: K2, m1, p2 tog, k8, p3, (k1, p4) twice, k1, p3, k8, m1, p2 tog, k2.

Row 33: K2, m1, p2 tog, k2, m1, (p2 tog) 3 times, m1, k1, k2 tog, p1, (k2 tog) twice, p1, (k2 tog) twice, p1, k2 tog, k1, m1, (p2 tog) 3 times, m1, k2, m1, p2 tog, k2.

Row 34: K2, m1, p2 tog, k7, p2, (k1, p2) 3 times, k7, m1, p2 tog, k2.

Row 35: K2, m1, p2 tog, k2, m1, (k1, p1 in next st) m1, p3 tog, m1, (k1, p1 in next st) m1, k2 tog, p1, k2 tog, (p1, k2 tog) twice, m1, (k1, p1 in next st) m1, p3 tog, m1, (k1, p1, in next st) m1, k2, m1, p2 tog, k2.

Row 36: K2, m1, p2 tog, k11, (p1, k1) 3 times, p1, k11, m1, p2 tog, k2.

Row 37: K2, m1, p2 tog, k2, m1, p4, m1, p1, m1, p4, m1, k3 tog, p1, k3 tog, m1, p4, m1, p1, m1, p4, m1, k2, m1, p2 tog, k2.

Row 38: K2, m1, p2 tog, k15, p1, k1, p1, k15, m1, p2 tog, k2.

Row 39: K2, m1, p2 tog, k2, m1, (p2 tog) 3 times, m1, p1, m1, (p2 tog) 3 times, m1, k3 tog, m1, (p2 tog) 3 times, m1, p1, m1, (p2 tog) 3 times, m1, k2, m1, p2 tog, k2.

Row 40: K2, m1, p2 tog, k27, m1, p2 tog, k2.

Row 41: K2, m1, p2 tog, k2, m1, (k1, p1 in next st) m1, (p3 tog, m1) 3 times, (k1, p1 in next st) m1, p1, m1, (k1, p1 in next st) (m1 p3 tog) 3 times, m1, (k1, p1 in next st) m1, k2, m1, p2 tog, k2.

Row 42: K2, m1, p2 tog, k31, m1, p2 tog, k2.

Row 43: K2, m1, p2 tog, k2, m1, p4, m1, p2 tog, p1, p2 tog, m1, p4, m1, k1, m1, p4, m1, p2 tog, p1, p2 tog, m1, p4, m1, k2, m1,.
p2 tog, k2.

Row 44: K2, m1, p2 tog, k8, k3 tog, k6, p1, k6, k3 tog, k8, m1, p2 tog, k2.

Row 45: K2, m1, p2 tog, k2, m1, (p2 tog) 3 times, m1, p1, m1, (p2 tog) 3 times, m1, k1, m1, (p2 tog) 3 times, m1, p1, m1, (p2 tog) 3 times, m1, k2, m1, p2 tog, k2.

Row 46: K2, m1, p2 tog, k13, p1, k13, m1, p2 tog, k2.

Row 47: K2, m1, p2 tog, k2, m1, p1, (m1, p3 tog) 7 times, m1, p1, m1, k2, m1, p2 tog, k2.

Row 48: K2, m1, p2 tog, k2, p3, k2 tog, k1, k2 tog, m1, k3 tog, m1, k2 tog, k1, k2 tog, p3, k2, m1, p2 tog, k2.

Row 49: K2, m1, p2 tog, k2, m1, k3, m1, p3 tog, p3, p3 tog, m1, k3, m1, k2, m1, p2 tog, k2.

Row 50: K2, m1, p2 tog, k2, p5, k2 tog, k1, k2 tog, p5, k2, m1, p2 tog, k2.

Row 51: K2, m1, p2 tog, k2, m1, k5, m1, p3 tog, m1, k5, m1, k2, m1, p2 tog, k2.

Row 52: K2, m1, p2 tog, k2, p7, k1, p7, k2, m1, p2 tog, k2.

Row 53: K2, m1, p2 tog, k2, m1, k3, p1, k3, m1, p1, m1, k3, p1, k3, m1, k2, m1, p2 tog, k2.

Row 54: K2, m1, p2 tog, k2, p4, (k1, p4) 3 times, k2, m1, p2 tog, k2.

Row 55: K2, m1, p2 tog, k2, m1, k4, p1, k4, m1, k1, m1, k4, p1, k4, m1, k2, m1, p2 tog, k2.

Row 56: K2, m1, p2 tog, k2, p5, (k1, p5) 3 times, k2, m1, p2 tog, k2.

Row 57: K2, m1, p2 tog, k2, m1, k5, p1, k5, m1, p1, m1, k5, p1, k5, m1, k2, m1, p2 tog, k2.

Row 58: K2, m1, p2 tog, k2, p6, (k1, p6) 3 times, k2, m1, p2 tog, k2.

Row 59: K2, m1, p2 tog, k2, m1, k4, k2 tog, p1, k2 tog, k4, m1, p1, m1, k4, k2 tog, p1, k2 tog, k4, m1, k2, m1, p2 tog, k2.

Row 60: K2, m1, p2 tog, k2, p6, (k1, p6) 3 times, k2, m1, p2 tog, k2.

Repeat rows 1–60 until length desired, ending the lace on row 19.

Rows 1–60 form one complete pattern of Berry and Leaf Lace. The lace has been used in the following manner for the four panels in the skirt of the gown and around the width of the skirt, the front, left and right back of yoke. Proceed as follows for the instructions on the use of the lace used in the christening gown.

Berry and Leaf Lace insertion panels (make 4)

Cast on 39 sts.
Work Berry and Leaf Lace pattern rows 1–60, 4 times.
Work rows 1–14 once.
Cast off.

Berry and Leaf Lace insertion for skirt width.

Cast on 39 sts.
Work Berry and Leaf Lace pattern rows 1–60, 13 times.
Cast off. Join or graft ends together.

Front yoke

Cast on 39 sts.
Begin with row 9, work to row 60, then work rows 1–10.
End with rows 1–14.
Cast off.

Right back yoke

Cast on 39 sts.
Begin with row 9. Work to row 60, then rows 1–10.
Work 7 rows st, st.
Knit 2 rows.
Cast off.

Left back yoke

Cast on 39 sts. Knit 4 rows.
Rows 5, 7 and 9: Purl.
Rows 6 and 8: Knit.
Begin lace at row 11, work to row 60, then rows 1–12.
Cast off.

NARROW LACE EDGING

Cast on 5 sts.
Row 1: K2, m1, k1, m1, k2.
Row 2: Knit.
Row 3: K3, m1, k2 tog, m1, k2.
Row 4: Knit.
Row 5: K4, m1, k2 tog, m1, k2.
Row 6: Cast off 4 sts. K to end of row.

Sleeve edgings (make 4)

Work rows 1–6 of narrow lace edging. Repeat 20 times.
Cast off.

Narrow lace edging for sides of lace panels (make 8)

Work pattern rows 1–6, 42 times.

Narrow lace edging for skirt insertion

Work 2 lengths for both sides of skirt insertion.
Work lace edging until it measures across front and back of yoke, making the back piece in 2 separate lengths and working sufficient to edge both sides of the insertion.

UNDER LACE EDGING

Cast on 13 sts.
Row 1: Sl 1, k2, m1, k2 tog, k1, (m2, k2 tog) twice, k3.
Row 2: Sl 1, k4, p1, k2, p1, k3, m1, k2 tog, k1.
Row 3: Sl 1, k2, m1, k2 tog, k3, (m2, k2 tog) twice, k3.
Row 4: Sl 1, k4, p1, k2, p1, k5, m1, k2 tog, k1.
Row 5: Sl 1, k2, m1, k2 tog, k5, (m2, k2 tog) twice, k3.

Row 6: Sl 1, k4, p1, k2, p1, k7, m1, k2 tog, k1.
Row 7: Sl 1, k2, m1, k2 tog, k14.
Row 8: Sl 1, k15, m1, k2 tog, k1.
Row 9: Sl 1, k2, m1, k2 tog, k14.
Row 10: As row 8.
Row 11: As row 9.
Row 12: Cast off 6 sts. K to last 3 sts, m1, k2 tog, k1.
Repeat rows 1–12 until length required to fit around lower skirt edge of insertion lace. The under lace edging is designed to lift the narrow lace edging and to give the hemline an attractive appearance.

To make up christening gown

Stitch narrow lace edging to both sides of the lace panels. Fold over and make a 2 cm (¾″) hem on shoulder pieces and stitch into place on front and back yoke. Join front and back panels to lace insertion, then to side panels. Fold over 2 cm (¾″) on shoulder pieces. Stitch into place on front and back yoke. Stitch yoke to skirt. Sew in sleeves. Attach narrow lace edging to cast-on edge and to one row above the ribbon holes in sleeves. Stitch lace insertion around bottom of the gown. Sew under lace to edge and narrow lace to both sides of insertion. Thread ribbon through sleeves. Make four loops on back yoke of gown. Sew on small flat buttons to correspond. To trim the gown make 14 rosettes.

Rosettes

Cast on 4 sts.
Row 1: K1, m1, k1, m1, k2.
Row 2: Knit.
Row 3: K2, m1, k2 tog, m1, k2.
Row 4: Knit.
Row 5: K3, m1, k2 tog, m1, k2.
Row 6: Cast off 4 sts. K to end of row.
Repeat rows 1–6 seven times.
Cast off.
Join ends. Gather to form rosette. Work pink stamens with DMC stranded cotton. Attach a rosette to each side of lace panels at skirt edge (8 rosettes). Sew a rosette in the centre of each lace panel at yoke (4 rosettes). Place a rosette above the ribbon bow on the sleeves (2 rosettes).

BONNET

Back

Cast on 6 sts (2 sts on each of 3 needles). Work with 4th needle.
Round 1: (M1, k1) to end of round.

Round 2 and alternate rounds: Knit unless otherwise indicated.

Round 3: (M1, k2) to end of round.

Round 5: (M1, k3) to end of round.

Round 7: (M1, k4) to end of round.

Continue increasing in this manner, knitting an extra st between sections until there are 32 sts on each needle (96 sts).

Round 33: (M1, k1, m1, sl 1, k1, psso, k13) to end of round.

Round 35: (M1, k3, m1, sl 1, k1, psso, k12) to end of round.

Round 37: (M1, k5, m1, sl 1, k1, psso, k11) to end of round.

Round 39: (M1, k7, m1, sl 1, k1, psso, k10) to end of round.

Round 41: (M1, k9, m1, sl 1, k1, psso, k9) to end of round.

Round 43: (M1, k11, m1, sl 1, k1, psso, k8) to end of round.

Round 45: (M1, k13, m1, sl 1, k1, psso, k7) to end of round.

Round 47: (M1, k15, m1, sl 1, k1, psso, k6) to end of round.

Round 49: (M1, k17, m1, sl 1, k1, psso, k5) to end of round.

Round 51: (M1, k19, m1, sl 1, k1, psso, k4) to end of round.

Round 53: (M1, k21, m1, sl 1, k1, psso, k3) to end of round.

Round 55: (M1, k23, m1, sl 1, k1, psso, k2) to end of round.

Detail of Ruth Evelyn showing bonnet and bootees.

Round 57: (M1, k25, m1, sl 1, k1, psso, k1) to end of round.
Round 59: (M1, k27, m1, k2 tog) to end of round.
Knit 2 rounds.
Round 62: Knit across 2 needles. Cast off half of the sts on 3rd needle for back of neck.
Now work in rows.
Row 63: Knit.
Cast off purlwise.

Front

Cast on 39 sts. Work Berry and Leaf Lace rows 1–60 twice, then rows 1–36 (page 15).
Cast off.
Work a length of Narrow Lace Edging rows 1–6, until length required to edge front, back and sides on Berry and Leaf Lace insertion. Join bonnet back to lace insertion. Stitch lace edging around lace. Stitch ribbon ties into place. Attach a rosette (make 2) each side.

BOOTEES

Make 2.

Cast on 43 sts.
Row 1: K1, k twice in next st, k18, k twice in next st, k1, k twice in next st, k18, k twice in next st, k1.
Row 2 and every alternate row: Knit.
Row 3: K1, k twice in next st, k20, k twice in next st, k1, k twice in next st, k20, k twice in next st, k1. Continue increasing in this manner until there are 75 sts on the needle.
Work 14 rows st, st. Continue thus:.
Row 18: K43, k2 tog. Turn.
Row 19: * Sl 1, p11, p2 tog. Turn.
Row 20: K12, k2 tog *.
Repeat *–* until there are 49 sts on the needle. Purl to end of row.
Continue thus:
Purl 2 rows.

Row 3: Knit.
Row 4: Purl.
Row 5: K1, (m2, k2 tog, k1) to end of row.
Row 6: Purl (dropping 1 loop of m2 of the previous row).
Row 7: Purl.
Row 8: Knit.
Row 9: Purl.
Cast off.
For each bootee knit 2 lengths of Narrow Lace Edging, one to go around instep and one to sew under ribbon holes. Work a length of Under Lace to sew around the top of each bootee. Join back seams. Sew on laces. Make 2 rosettes and attach to toes. Thread ribbon through holes.

HANDKERCHIEF

Cast on 13 sts.
Work a length of Under Lace Edging to trim the handkerchief.
Cast off.
Join ends of lace using fine sts.

PILLOW SLIP

Cast on 144 sts.
Work 6 rows st, st.
Row 7: K2, (m2, k2 tog, k2). Repeat to last 4 sts, m2, k2 tog, k2.
Row 8: Purl (dropping 1 loop of the m2 of the previous row).
Rows 9–15: St, st.
Cast off.
Work a length of Narrow Lace Edging and attach to st st ribbon hole strip. Sew across top of pillow slip at opening. Thread ribbon through holes and secure. Work a length of Under Lace Edging and sew around pillow slip, allowing fullness at corners. Make a rosette as before. Attach to ribbon hole strip at the corner. Press the pillow slip.

2: MIMOSA

A dainty eyelet dress with a laced closure at the neck was knitted by Edna Lomas from a 1930s design. It is worn by Natalie Carbone aged 15 months.

Materials

3 × 50 g balls DMC 20 cotton
Needles 3 mm (11)
Length of fine crochet or knitted cord for neck

Measurements

Underarm 61 cm (24″)
Neck to hem 43 cm (17″)
Sleeve 9 cm (3½″)
Tension 8 sts to 2.5 cm (1″)

Front

Cast on 153 sts. (Do not knit into back of cast-on sts.)
Work 14 rows st, st.

Next row: Purl.
Work in pattern thus:
Row 1: K1, * p3, k6. Repeat from * to last 5 sts, k5.
Row 2: P5, * k1, m1, k2 tog, p6. Repeat from * to last st, p1.
Row 3: As row 1.
Row 4: Purl.
Row 5: K5, * p3, k6. Repeat from * to last 4 sts, p3, k1.
Row 6: P1, * k1, m1, k2 tog, p6. Repeat from * to last 5 sts, p5.
Row 7: As row 5.
Row 8: Purl.
Repeat rows 1–8 until work measures approx. 30 cm (12″) or length required. End with purl row.
Next row: Work waistband thus:
K7, * k2 tog. Repeat from * to last 6 sts, k6 (83 sts).
Work 9 rows moss st, knitting 2 tog at end of 9th row (82 sts).
Next row: Cast off 3 sts, k to end of row.
Next row: Cast off 3 sts, p to end of row.
Next row: K2 tog, k to last 2 sts, k2 tog.
Next row: P37. Turn.
Work on these 37 sts for right half of front bodice thus (place the other 37 sts on st holder until required):
Row 1: K1, * p3, k6. Repeat from * to end of row.
Row 2: P6, * k1, m1, k2 tog, p6. Repeat from * until last 4 sts, k1, m1, k2 tog, p1.
Row 3: As row 1.
Row 4: Purl.
Row 5: K5, * p3, k6. Repeat from * to last 11 sts, k11.
Row 6: P11, * k1, m1, k2 tog, p6. Repeat from * to last 5 sts, p5.
Row 7: As Row 5.
Row 8: Purl.
Repeat these 8 rows until work measures 9 cm (3½″) from underarm (end with purl row).

Next row: Cast off 13 sts. K to end of row.
Work 6 rows st, st, knitting 2 tog at neck in first 4 rows (20 sts). Cast off.
Return to the 37 sts on holder. Join yarn at front opening.
Purl to end of row.
Proceed as follows:
Row 1: K6, * p3, k6. Repeat from * to last 4 sts, p3, k1.
Row 2: P1, * k1, m1, k2 tog, p6. Repeat from * to end of row.
Row 3: As row 1.
Row 4: Purl.
Row 5: K11, * p3, k6. Repeat from * to last 5 sts, k5.
Row 6: P5, * k1, m1, k2 tog, p6. Repeat from * until last 11 sts, p11.
Row 7: As row 5.
Row 8: Purl.
Repeat last 8 rows until work measures 9 cm (3½″). End with knit row.
Cast off 13 sts. P to end.
Work 6 rows st, st, knitting 2 tog at neck in first 4 rows.
Cast off.

Back

Work as front until you have completed armhole shaping (74 sts).
Now work 8 pattern rows, knitting the 1st and last st in each row. When bodice measures 10 cm (4″) from underarm, continue the shaping by casting off 10 sts at beginning of next 4 rows.
Cast off.

Sleeves (both alike)

Cast on 41 sts.
Work 9 rows moss st.
Next row: K5, (k1, p1) in every st until 5 sts remain, k5 (72 sts).
Next row: Purl.
Work 8 rows of skirt pattern until sleeve measures 7.5 cm (3″) from beginning.
Shape top of sleeve by casting off 3 sts at beginning of every row, keeping continuity of pattern, until 42 sts remain.
Next row: K1, * k2 tog, k1. Repeat from * to end of row.
Cast off.

Collar

Cast on 97 sts.
Work 4 rows moss st.
Next row: Moss st 3, k2 tog, k to last 3 sts, moss st 3.
Next row: Moss st 3, p to last 3 sts, moss st 3.

Work 8 rows of skirt pattern, keeping 3 moss sts at both ends of every row.

Row 9: Moss st 3, * k8, k2 tog. Repeat from * to last 3 sts, moss st.

Work 4 rows st, st.

Row 14: Moss st 3, * p7, p2 tog. Repeat from * to last 3 sts, moss st 3.

Work 2 rows st, st.

Cast off.

To make up

Press the work carefully on the wrong side under a damp cloth. Join shoulders. Sew side seams. Sew sleeve seam. Sew in sleeves, placing seam to seam. Work dc around neck and front opening. Sew on collar. Make a length of knitted or crochet cord to lace the front opening. Trim ends of cord with pompoms or tassels if desired.

Turn up a narrow hem on skirt and slip stitch into place.

3. POSY

Hand embroidery by Joan Jackson adds colour to a diamond bobbled dress knitted by Edna Lomas. Posy is suitable for a two to three year old. Lengths of dress and sleeves are easily adjusted where indicated in the instructions. The skirt hangs from the embroidered yoke, allowing fullness in the design. Posy is worn here by two year old Jessica Stamatis.

Materials

Approx 7 × 50 g balls 4-ply cotton
Needles 3.25 mm (10) and 2.75 mm (12)
4 small buttons
DMC stranded embroidery thread, colours nos 221, 223, 224, 225, 501, 502, 522 (see Garlands pattern, page 32, for details)

Measurements

Underarm 66 cm (26″)
Neck to hem 53 cm (21″)
Sleeves 5 cm (2″)
Tension 7 sts to 2.5 cm (1″) over st, st

Front

Cast on 179 sts using 3.25 mm (10) needles.
Row 1: Knit.
Row 2: K1, p to last st, k1.
Repeat rows 1 and 2 once.
Row 5: K1, * m1, k2 tog. Repeat from * to end of row.
Row 6: K1, p to last st, k1.
Repeat rows 1 and 2 twice.
Row 11: Form hem by knitting 1st of cast-on edge to 1st on needle.
Row 12: K1, k 7 times into next st (working alternately into back and front of the st). Slip the 7 loops from RH needle on to LH needle. Knit into back of the 7 loops, slipping the one loop onto RH needle (this action will be referred to as mb in the instructions) * p15, mb. Repeat from * to last st, k1.
Rows 13 and 15: Knit.
Row 14: K1, p to last st, k1.
Row 16: K1, p2, * mb, p11, mb, p3 *. Repeat from *–* to last st, k1.
Work 3 rows st, st.
Row 20: K1, p4, mb, * p7, mb. Repeat from * to last 5 sts, p4, k1.
Work 3 rows st, st.
Row 24: K1, p6, mb, p3, mb, * p11, mb, p3, mb. Repeat from * to last 7 sts, p6, k1.
Work 3 rows st, st.
Row 28: K1, p8, mb, * p15, mb. Repeat from * to last 9 sts, p8, k1.
Work 3 rows st, st.
Row 32: As row 24.
Work 3 rows st, st.
Row 36: As row 20.
Work 3 rows st, st.
Row 40: As row 16.
Work 3 rows st, st.
Row 44: As row 12.

Continue in st, st until work measures 29 cm (11½″) from hemline, ending with purl row (adjust length if desired).
Next row: K2 tog to last st, k1 (90 sts).
Continue in pattern thus:
Row 1: K1, p4, mb, * p15, mb. Repeat from * to last 4 sts, p3, inc 1 in last st.
Work 3 rows st, st.
Row 5: K1, p6, mb, p11, mb, * p3, mb, p11, mb. Repeat from * to last 7 sts, p6, k1.
Work 3 rows st, st.
Row 9: K1, p8, * mb, p7. Repeat from * to last st, k1.
Work 3 rows st, st.
Row 13: K1, p10, mb, p3, mb, * p11, mb, p3, mb. Repeat from * to last 11 sts, p10, k1.
Work 3 rows st, st.
Row 17: K1, p12, mb, * p15, mb. Repeat from * to last 13 sts, p12, k1.
Work 3 rows st, st.
Row 21: As row 13.
Work 3 rows st, st.
Row 25: As row 9.

Armhole

Keeping continuity of pattern, cast off 5 sts at beginning of next 2 rows. Decrease 1 st each end of needle in every row until there are 71 sts on needle. Continue in pattern without shaping until 49 pattern rows have been worked.
Next row: K25 sts. Cast off 21 sts. K to end of row.
Work on last 25 sts as follows:
Dec 1 st at neck edge of every alternate row until 21 sts remain. Continue on these 21 sts in pattern until armhole measures 12.5 cm (5″). Cast off 7 sts on each alternate row 3 times. Join in yarn where sts were left. Work to correspond with other side.

Back

Work as front until 71 sts remain.
Continue in pattern without shaping until armhole measures same as front.
Next row: K25 sts. Cast off 21 sts. K to end of row.
Cast off 7 sts at beginning of every alternate row and at the same time k2 tog at neck edge of every row.
Join yarn to where sts were left. Work to correspond with other shoulder

Sleeves

Cast on 57 sts.
Work rows 1–11 inclusive as for front.

Row 12: K1, p19, inc 1st in next 16 sts, p to last st, k1 (73 sts).
Work 5 rows st, st.
Continue pattern thus:
Row 1: K1, p35, mb, p35, k1.
Work 3 rows st, st.
Row 5: K1, p33, mb, p3, mb, p to last st, k1.
Work 3 rows st, st dec 1 st at beginning of each row.
Row 9: K2 tog, p29, mb, p7, mb, p to last st, k1.
Work 3 rows st, st dec 1 st at beginnning of each row.
Row 13: K2 tog, p25, mb, p11, mb, p to last st, k1.
Work 3 rows st, st dec 1 st at beginning of each row.
Row 17: K2 tog, p21, mb, p15, mb, p to last st, k1.
Work 3 rows st, st dec 1 st at beginning of each row.
Row 21: K2 tog, p21, mb, p11, mb, p to last st, k1.
Work 3 rows st, st dec 1 st at beginning of each row.
Row 25: K2 tog, p21, mb, p7, mb, p to last st, k1.
Work 3 rows st, st dec 1 st at beginning of each row.
Row 29: K2 tog, p21, mb, p3, mb, p to last st, k1.
Work 3 rows st, st dec 1 st at beginning of each row.
Row 33: K2 tog, p21, mb, p to last st, k1.
Continue in st, st dec 1 st at beginning of each row until 25 sts remain.
Cast off.

Neckband

Sew up right shoulder seam. Sew left shoulder for approximately 2.5 cm (1″) from shoulder to partially close seam.
Using 2.75 mm (12) needles with right side of work facing, pick up and knit 96 sts around neck. Work k1, p1, rib for 6 rows.
Cast off ribwise.

Make up

Lightly press work before joining seams and embroider flowers and leaves in each diamond. Sew up side and sleeve seams. Sew in sleeves, adjusting gathering evenly at the top to fit armholes. Work 2 rows of dc around shoulder opening. Make 4 loop buttonholes in 2nd row on front shoulder. Sew on buttons to correspond with loops.

4. ALEXIS

A 1920s style dress worn by two year old Jessica Stamatis. The longer length and half belt give a tailored look set off by the modish cloche hat. Edna Lomas knitted this attractive garment.

Materials

8 balls 4-ply cotton
Needles 3 mm (11) and 3.75 mm (9)
2 buttons for belt

Measurements

Underarm 66 cm (26″)
Neck to hem 56 cm (22″)
Sleeve 20 cm (8″)
Tension 6 sts to 2.5 cm (1″) over st, st

Special abbreviations for this pattern

Inc 1 = pick up horizontal loop lying before next st.
  Work into back of loop.
c4 = slip next 2 sts on cable needle to front of work, k2,
  then k2 from cable needle.

Back

Using 3 mm (11) needles cast on 130 sts.
Work 4 rows k1, p1, rib.
Next row: Rib 4, inc 1, * rib 3, inc 1. Repeat from * to
last 3 sts, rib 3 (172 sts).
Change to 3.75 mm (9) needles. Continue thus:
Row 1: Wrong side facing, k4, p4, * k6, p4. Repeat from
* to last 4 sts, k4.
Row 2: P4, c4, * p6, c4. Repeat from * to last 4 sts, p4.
Row 3: As row 1.
Row 4: P4, k4, * p6, k4. Repeat from * to last 4 sts, p4.
Repeat rows 1–4 twice.

Shape as follows:
Row 1: K4, p4, * k2, k2 tog, k2, p4. Repeat from * to
last 4 sts, k4 (156 sts).
Next row: P4, c4, * p5, c4. Repeat from * to last 4 sts, p4.
Keeping pattern correct work 10 rows straight.

2nd shaping row:
K1, k2 tog, k1, p4, * k1, k2 tog, k2, p4. Repeat from
* to last 4 sts, k1, k2 tog, k1 (138 sts).
Next row: P3, c4, * p4, c4. Repeat from * to last 3 sts, p3.
Keeping pattern correct work 10 rows straight.

3rd shaping row:
K3, p4, * k1, k2 tog, k1, p4. Repeat from * to last 3
sts, k3 (122 sts).
Next row: P3, * c4, p3. Repeat from * to end of row.
Keeping pattern correct work 10 rows straight.

4th shaping row:
K1, k2 tog, * p4, k2 tog, k1. Repeat from * to end of
row (104 sts).

Next row: P2, * c4, p2. Repeat from * to end of row.
Keeping pattern correct work 10 rows straight.
Next row: P1, (p2 tog, p1) 6 times, * p2 tog, p2. Repeat
from * to last 21 sts, (p2 tog, p1) 7 times (75 sts).
Next row: Continue in st, st, beginning with knit row,
until back measures 37 cm (14½″) or length desired
(measured up the centre back), ending with right side
facing.

Shape raglans:
Cast off 2 sts at beginning of next 2 rows, then decrease
1 st both ends of next and every alternate row until 25
sts remain. Knit 1 row. Leave sts on holder.

Front

Using 3 mm (11) needles, cast on 106 sts.
Work 4 rows k1, p1, rib.
Next row: Rib 2, inc 1, (rib 3, inc 1) 7 times, rib 11, inc
1, (rib 3, inc 1) 13 times, rib 10, inc 1, (rib 3, inc 1)
7 times, rib 2 (136 sts).
Change to 3.75 mm (9) needles. Continue thus:
Row 1: Wrong side facing, k4, p4, (k6, p4) twice, k4,
p10, k4, p4, (k6, p4) 4 times, k4, p10, k4, p4, (k6, p4)
twice, k4.
Row 2: P4, c4, (p6, c4) twice, p4, k10, p4, c4, (p6, c4)
4 times, p4, k10, p4, c4, (p6, c4) twice, p4.
Row 3: As row 1.
Row 4: P4, k4, (p6, k4) twice, p4, k10, p4, k4, (p6, k4)
4 times, p4, k10, p4, k4, (p6, k4) twice, p4.
Repeat rows 1–4 twice.

Shape as follows:
K4, p4, (k2, k2 tog, k2, p4) twice, k4, p10, k4, p4, (k2,
k2 tog, k2, p4) 4 times, k4, p10, k4, p4, (k2, k2 tog,
k2, p4) twice, k4 (128 sts).
Keeping pattern correct work 11 rows straight.

2nd shaping row:
K1, k2 tog, k1, p4, (k1, k2 tog, k2, p4) twice, k1, k2
tog, k1, p10, k1, k2 tog, k1, p4, (k1, k2 tog, k2, p4) 4
times, k1, k2 tog, k1, p10, k1, k2 tog, k1, p4, (k1, k2
tog, k2, p4) twice, k1, k2 tog, k1 (114 sts).
Keeping pattern correct work 11 rows straight.

3rd shaping row:
K3, p4, (k1, k2 tog, k1, p4) twice, k3, p10, k3, p4, (k1,
k2 tog, k1, p4) 4 times, k3, p10, k3, p4, (k1, k2 tog,
k1, p4) twice, k3 (106 sts).
Keeping pattern correct work 11 rows straight.

4th shaping row:
K1, k2 tog, (p4, k2 tog, k1) 3 times, p10, k1, k2 tog,
(p4, k2 tog, k1) 5 times, p10, k1, k2 tog, (p4, k2 tog,
k1) 3 times (92 sts).

Keeping pattern correct work 11 rows straight.
Next row: (P2, p2 tog) 5 times, p10, k2, (p4, k2) 5 times, p10, (p2 tog, p2) 5 times (82 sts).
Next row: K25, p2, (c4, p2) 5 times, k25.
Keeping centre 32 sts in pattern and remaining sts in st, st work straight until front matches back to start of raglan shaping, ending with right side facing.

Shape raglans
Cast off 2 sts at beginning of next 2 rows, then decrease 1 st both ends of next and every alternate row until 44 sts remain.

Shape neck as follows:
Next row: Work 13, turn leaving remaining sts on spare needle.
Continue on these sts for first side as follows:
Continue to decrease 1 st at raglan edge as before on next and every alternate row, at the same time decreasing 1 st at neck edge on every row, until 5 sts remain. Keeping neck edge straight continue decreasing at raglan edge as before until all sts are gone with wrong side facing. Slip centre 18 sts on a spare needle. Rejoin yarn to remaining 13 sts. Work to end, finish to correspond with first side.

Sleeves

Using 3 mm (11) needles, cast on 38 sts.
Work 5 cm (2″) k1, p1, rib.
Next row: Rib 4, inc 1, (rib 10, inc 1) 3 times, rib 4 (42 sts).
Change to 3.75 mm (9) needles. Work in st, st, shaping sides by increasing 1 st both ends of 3rd and every following 7th row until there are 56 sts.
Work straight until sleeve seam measures 23 cm (9″), ending with right side facing.
Shape raglans by casting off 2 sts at beginning of next 2 rows, then decrease 1 st each end of next and every alternate row until 6 sts remain.
Work 1 row straight. Leave sts on holder.

Belt

Using 3 mm (11) needles, cast on 13 sts.
Work in k1, p1, rib as follows:
Row 1: Right side facing, k2, (p1, k1) 5 times, k1.
Row 2: K1, (p1, k1) 6 times.
Repeat rows 1 and 2 twice.
Make buttonholes as follows:
Rib 5, cast off 3 sts. Rib to end and back, casting on 3 sts over those cast off.
Continue straight in rib until belt measures 43 cm (17″) (adjust belt length here).
Make another buttonhole as before. Rib 6 rows.
Cast off ribwise.

To make up

Using cool iron and dry cloth press dress sections lightly on wrong side. Join raglan seams on left sleeve and front raglan on right sleeve.

Neckband

With right side facing and using 3 mm (11) needles, work as follows:
K25 from back; k6 from sleeve; pick up and knit 12 sts down left side of neck. Knit across sts at centre front, decreasing 1 st at centre. Pick up and knit 12 sts up right side of neck; k6 sleeve sts (78 sts).
Work 5 cm (2″) k1, p1, rib.
Cast off loosely ribwise.

To finish

Join remaining raglan seam then join neckband using a flat seam.
Fold neckband in half to wrong side and loosely slip stitch hem in position. Join side and sleeve seams. Press the seams. Sew on buttons and belt.

5: JESSICA

A classic coat dress with a detachable collar and hem lace, designed and knitted by Eileen Kerney, worn by Jessica Stamatis. The dress is suitable for a two year old. The length can be adjusted where indicated in the pattern.

Materials

Dress: 5 × 50 g balls 4-ply wool.
Needles 2.75 mm (12), 3 mm (11) and 3.25 mm (10).
Hem lace: 1 × 50 g ball white 4-ply cotton
Needles 2.50 mm (13)
Collar: 1 × 20 g ball DMC 20 cotton
Needles 2 mm (14)
8 pearl buttons for dress
1 small pearl button for collar

Measurements

Underarm 56 cm (22″)
Neck to hem 43 cm (17″)
Sleeves 19 cm (7½″)
Tension 7½ sts to 2.5 cm (1″) over st, st

Back

Using 3 mm (11) needles, cast on 145 sts.
** Beginning with knit row work 9 rows st, st.
Next row: Knit (forms hem ridge).
Change to 3.25 mm (10) needles.
Beginning with knit row, continue in st, st until work measures 20 cm (8″) or length desired from hem ridge, ending after a knit row **.

Work decreasing thus:
P11, (p2 tog) 62 times, p10 (83 sts).
Continue in rib thus:
Row 1: K1, * p1, k1. Repeat from * to end of row.
Row 2: P1, * k1, p1. Repeat from * to end of row.
Repeat last 2 rows for 4 cm (1½″), ending after a 2nd row.

Shape armholes:
Cast off 16 sts ribwise at beginning of next 2 rows (51 sts).
Continue in rib until back measures 34 cm (13½″), ending after a 2nd rib row.

Shape shoulders:
Cast off 9 sts at start of next 2 rows (33 sts). Break off yarn, leave sts on holder.

Left front

Using 3 mm (11) needles, cast on 73 sts.
Work as for back from **–**.

Decreasing row:
P7, (p2 tog) 30 times, p6 (43 sts).

Continue in rib as for back for 4 cm (1½″) ending after 2nd row (for the right front end after a 1st row).

Shape armhole:
Cast off 16 sts at beginning of next row (27 sts). Continue in rib until front measures 29 cm (11½″) from hem ridge, ending after a 1st rib row (for right front, end after a 2nd row).

Shape neck:
Cast off 7 sts at beginnning of next row and following alternate row. Decrease 1 st at neck edge on every row until 9 sts remain. Continue without further shaping until front measures same as back to shoulders, ending after a 2nd rib row.
Cast off.

Right front

Work as for left front, noting the variations in brackets.

Sleeves

Using 2.75 mm (12) needles, cast on 51 sts.
Work in k1, p1, rib until work measures 4 cm (1½″) from cast-on edge, ending after wrong side row and increasing 10 sts evenly across last row (61 sts).

Change to 3.25 mm (10) needles.
Beginning with knit row continue in st, st, at the same time increasing 1 st at each end of 7th row and every following 10th row until there are 69 sts on needle.
Continue without further shaping until sleeve measures 16 cm (6¼″) from cast-on edge, ending after a purl row and increasing 3 sts evenly across last row (72 sts).
Work 22 rows st, st.
Cast off.

Neckband

Join shoulder seams. With right side facing and using 2.75 mm (12) needles, pick up and knit 27 sts up right front. Knit sts from back neck, increasing 4 sts evenly across. Pick up and knit 27 sts down left front (91 sts).
Work in k1, p1, rib for 8 rows.
Cast off ribwise.

Buttonhole band

Join side seams. Fold hems to wrong side along ridge. Slip st into place. With right side of work facing and using 2.75 mm (12) needles, pick up and knit 104 sts evenly up right front.

Row 1: K2, * p1, k1. Repeat from * to last 2 sts, k2.
Row 2: K2, * p1, k1. Repeat from * to last 2 sts, k2.
Row 3: As row 1.

Work buttonholes thus:
Work 4, * cast off 2 sts. Rib until there are 14 sts on right-hand needle after cast off. Repeat from * 5 times. Cast off 2 sts. Work to end.
Next row: As row 1, casting on 2 sts over those cast off (forming buttonhole).
Next row: Work in rib.
Cast off ribwise.

Collar

Cast on 29 sts.
Row 1: K5, p16, (m1, k2 tog) 3 times, m1, k2.
Row 2: K25 turn.
Row 3: P17, (m1, k2 tog) 3 times, m1, k2.
Row 4: K26 turn.
Row 5: K18, (m1, k2 tog) 3 times, m1, k2.
Row 6: K9, p18, turn.
Row 7: K19, (m1, k2 tog) 3 times, m1, k2.
Row 8: K9, p19, k5.
Row 9: Knit.
Row 10: Cast off 4 sts, knit to end of row.
Repeat rows 1–10 until length desired.
Cast off.
Make a tiny loop at collar edge. Sew on small pearl button.

Hem lace

Cast on 8 sts.
Row 1: Sl 1, k5, m1, k2.
Row 2: M1, k2 tog, k7.
Row 3: Sl 1, k4, m1, k2 tog, m1, k2.
Row 4: M1, k2 tog, k8.
Row 5: Sl 1, k3, (m1, k2 tog) twice, m1, k2.
Row 6: M1, k2 tog, k9.
Row 7: Sl 1, k2, (m1, k2 tog) 3 times, m1, k2.
Row 8: M1, k2 tog, k10.
Row 9: Sl 1, k2, k2 tog, (m1, k2 tog) 3 times, k1.
Row 10: M1, k2 tog, k9.
Row 11: Sl 1, k3, k2 tog, (m1, k2 tog) twice, k1.
Row 12: M1, k2 tog, k8.
Row 13: Sl 1, k4, k2 tog, m1, k2 tog, k1.
Row 14: M1, k2 tog, k7.
Row 15: Sl 1, k5, k2 tog, k1.
Row 16: M1, k2 tog, k6.
Repeat rows 1–16 until length desired.

To make up

Press work lightly. Join sleeve seams. Fold sleeves in half lengthwise. Place centre of sleeve to shoulder seams. Match seams underarm.
Sew on buttons.
Attach length of lace under hemline. Tie white collar into position.

6. GARLANDS

A party dress knitted by Edna Lomas and embroidered by Joan Jackson. The dress is an A-line design, defined by panels of eyelets. Ribbon could be threaded through eyelets if desired. This dress is suitable for a two year old and allows ample room for growth. The sleeves are roomy with a late 1930s look. Dress is worn by two year old Annika Hellsing.

Materials

6 × 50 g balls 4-ply cotton
Needles 3.25 mm (10) and 2.75 mm (12)
Press studs and ribbon.
DMC stranded cotton, in colours Nos 221, 223, 224, 225, 501, 502, 522
For embroidery stitches see the chart in the pattern Berceuse, page 84.

Measurements

Underarm 66 cm (26″)
Neck to hem 51 cm (20″)
Sleeve 7.5 cm (3″)
Tension 7 sts to 2.5 cm (1″) over st, st

Back

Cast on 168 sts using 3.25 mm (10) needles.
Work 12 rows st, st.
Next row: K2, * m1, k2 tog, k1. Repeat from * to last st, k1.
Next row: Purl.
Work 4 rows st, st.
Next row: K39, * sl 1, k2 tog, psso, m1, k2, m1, k3 tog, k74. Repeat from * ending row with k39.
Work 5 rows st, st commencing and ending with a purl row.
Next row: K38, * sl 1, k2 tog, psso, m1, k2, m1, k3 tog, k72. Repeat from * ending row with k38.
Work 5 rows st, st.
Next row: K37, * sl 1, k2 tog, psso, m1, k2, m1, k3 tog, k70. Repeat from * ending row with k37.
Continue this way. Dec every 6th row, having 1 st less each end of the row, 2 sts less in centre panel, until there are 96 sts on needle.
Shape armholes by casting off 6 sts at beginning of next 2 rows.
K2 tog each end of the next 3 rows (78 sts).
Next row: K13, sl 1, k1, psso, m1, k2, m1, k3 tog, k23.
Leave remaining 35 sts on spare needle.
Work 5 rows st, st.
Next row: K13, sl 1, k1, psso, m1, k2, m1, k3 tog, k22.
Continue in this way, having 1 st less at centre back every 6th row until there are 36 sts on needle. When armhole measures 11.5 cm (4½″), shape shoulder by casting off 7 sts at armhole edge every 2nd row 3 times. Cast off.
Join yarn at centre back. Cast on 8 sts.
Next row: K23, sl 1, k2 tog, psso, m1, k2, m1, k2 tog, k13.
Work 5 rows st, st keeping 4 of the cast-on sts at centre back in garter st to form border.
Work to correspond with other side.

Front

Work as for back until armhole shaping is complete.
Next row: K13, sl 1, k1, psso, m1, k2, m1, k3 tog, k38, sl 1, k2 tog, psso, m1, k2, m1, k2 tog, k13.
Work 5 rows, st, st.
Next row: K13, sl 1, k1, psso, m1, k2, m1, k3 tog, k36, sl 1, k2 tog, psso, m1, k2, m1, k2 tog, k13.
Continue to work 5 rows st, st and dec 2 sts every 6th row until there are 66 sts on needle.
Next row: P28 (leave on spare needle), cast off 10 sts, p28.
Continue on last 28 sts, working 1 more decrease on the 6th row, and k2 tog at neck edge every row until there are 21 sts on needle.
When armhole measures 11.5 cm (4½″), shape shoulder by casting off 7 sts at armhole edge every 2nd row 3 times.
Join yarn at neck edge.
Work other side to correspond.

Sleeves

Using 3.25 mm (10) needles, cast on 75 sts.
Work 2.5 cm (1″) in moss st.
Next row: * K1, k2 tog. Repeat from * to end of row (50 sts). Change to 2.75 mm (12) needles. Work in k1, p1, rib for 2 cm (¾″).
Next row: * K1, k twice in next st. Repeat from * to end of row (75 sts).
Next row: Purl.
Change to 3.25 mm (10) needles.
Work in st, st for 2.5 cm (1″), then k2 tog each end of every 2nd row until there are 25 sts on needle.
Cast off.

Collar (make 2)

Using 3.25 mm (10) needles, cast on 51 sts.
Work in moss st for 4 cm (1½″).
Next row: Work in moss st, knitting every 3rd and 4th st tog.
Cast off.

To make up

Press with warm iron under damp cloth. Sew seams. Gather tops of sleeves. Sew on collar. Work 1 row dc round collar and back opening. Sew on press studs to close back. Make 2 cm (¾″) hem around lower edge. Embroider front and hemline as desired, following stitch diagram for Berceuse on page 84.

7. FERN

A delicate cotton dress knitted by Edna Lomas and worn by fifteen month old Natalie Carbone. The length of the dress and the sleeves can be adjusted to your requirements.

Materials

Approx. 5 × 20 g balls DMC 20 cotton
Needles 3 mm (11)
Length of narrow ribbon
Clear press studs

Measurements

Approx. chest measurement 56 cm (22")
Neck to hem 43 cm (17")
Sleeve 13 cm (approx 5¼")
Tension 7 sts to 2.5 cm (1") over moss st

Back

Cast on 141 sts using size 3 mm (11) needles.
Work 6 rows moss st.
Row 1: P1, k1, p1, * k2 tog, k5, (m1, k1, m1, k2) twice, sl 1, k1, psso, p1, k1, p1. Repeat from * to end of row.
Row 2 and alternate rows: P1, k1, p1, * p2 tog, p13, p2 tog, p1, k1, p1. Repeat from * to end of row.
Row 3: P1, k1, p1, * k2 tog, (k4, m1, k1, m1) twice, k1, sl 1, k1, psso, p1, k1, p1. Repeat from * to end of row.
Row 5: P1, k1, p1, * k2 tog, k3, m1, k1, m1, k6, m1, k1, m1, sl 1, k1, psso, p1, k1, p1. Repeat from * to end of row.
Row 7: P1, k1, p1, * k2 tog, (k2, m1, k1, m1) twice, k5, sl 1, k1, psso, p1, k1, p1. Repeat from * to end of row.
Row 9: P1, k1, p1, * k2 tog, k1, (m1, k1, m1, k4) twice, sl 1, k1, psso, p1, k1, p1. Repeat from * to end of row.
Row 11: P1, k1, p1, * k2 tog, m1, k1, m1, k6, m1, k1, m1, k3, sl 1, k1, psso, p1, k1, p1. Repeat from * to end of row.
Row 12: As row 2.
These 12 rows form fern pattern. Work until back measures 28 cm (11") or length desired.
Continue thus:.
Next row: (Right side of work), k7, * k2 tog. Repeat from * to last 8 sts, k8 (78 sts).

Smocking

Row 1: (Wrong side of work), p2, * k2, p4. Repeat from * to last 4 sts, k2, p2.
Row 2: K2, * sl 2, k4. Repeat from * to last 4 sts, sl 2, k2.
Row 3: P2, * sl 2, p4. Repeat from * to last 4 sts, sl 2, p2.
Row 4: * sl 2 on to spare needle (leave at back of work), k1. Knit the 2 sts from spare needle, sl 1 st on spare

needle, leave in front of work, k2, k the st from spare needle. Repeat from * to end of row.
Row 5: K1, * p4, k2. Repeat from * to last 5 sts, p4, k1.
Row 6: K1, * k4, sl 2. Repeat from * to last 5 sts, k5.
Row 7: P1, * p4, sl 2. Repeat from * to last 5 sts, p5.
Row 8: * Sl 1 st onto spare needle. Leave in front of work, k2. Knit the st from spare needle, sl 2 sts on spare needle and leave at back of work, k1. Knit the 2 sts from spare needle. Repeat from * to end of row.
Repeat rows 1–4.
Purl 1 row, p2 tog every 11th and 12th sts (72 sts).
Work in moss st, casting off 2 sts at beginning of next 2 rows (68 sts).
Next row: Moss st 36, leave remaining 32 sts on spare needle.
Continue in moss st on last 36 sts. When yoke measures 10 cm (4") cast off.
Join yarn at centre back, cast on 4 sts.
Work yoke to correspond with other side.

Front

Work as for back until the 12 rows of smocking have been completed. P1 row, p2 tog every 11th and 12th sts.
Continue in moss st.
Cast off 2 sts at beginning of next 2 rows.
Work until yoke measures 9 cm (3½"); continue thus:
Next row: Moss st 24 (leave on spare needle), cast off 20 sts, moss st 24. Continue on last 24 sts. K2 tog at neck edge every row until there are 20 sts on needle. Cast off.
Join yarn and work other side to correspond.

Sleeves (make 2)

Using 3 mm (11) needles, cast on 60 sts. Work in k1, p1, rib for 2.5 cm (1"). Work in fern lace pattern, omitting the 3 moss sts at beginning and end of each row. When sleeve measures 12.75 cm (5") or length desired, cast off 4 sts at beginning of every row until 20 sts remain Cast off.

Make up

Sew side and sleeve seams. Work 1 row dc around neck.
Next row: 3ch, * 1tr into next dc, 3ch. Miss 2dc.
Repeat from * to end of row.
Sew press studs on back opening. Thread ribbon through beading at neck if desired.

8. TALISMAN

An elegant christening gown from New Zealand made in the finest Swiss muslin. The dainty gown was sewn by Kathie Savage of Christchurch, and embroidered by Kathie using DMC thread in gold and white, one strand only. The Talisman Lace around neck and sleeves and the Ubique Leaf Lace at hem were knitted by the author, using DMC cotton 100 and 1 mm (20) needles. The gown is modelled by three months old Annalise O'Toole.

Materials

Approx. 2 × 20 g balls DMC cotton 100
Narrow silk ribbon
5 tiny buttons
A simple commercial pattern is ideal for the basic dress.
DMC stranded thread, gold and white

TALISMAN LACE

Cast on 9 sts.
Row 1: Sl 1, k1, m1, k2 tog, (m1, k1) 3 times, m1, k2.
Row 2: P13.
Row 3: Sl 1, k1, m1, k2 tog, m1, k3, m1, k1, m1, k3, m1, k2.

Row 4: P17.
Row 5: Sl 1, k1, m1, k2 tog, * m1, sl 1, (k2 tog) twice, pss and first k2 tog over the second k2 tog, m1, k1. Repeat from *, k1.
Row 6: Cast off 4 sts, p8.
Repeat rows 1–6 until length desired.

UBIQUE LEAF LACE

Cast on 28 sts.
Purl 1 row.
Row 1: Sl 1, k2, m1, k2 tog, k1, m1, k5, m1, sl 1, k2 tog, psso, m1, k5, m1, k3, m1, k2 tog, k4.
Row 2: K6, m1, k2 tog, p18, k1, m1, k2 tog, k1.

Details of Ubique Leaf Lace at neckline and sleeve

Detail of Talisman Lace at hem

Row 3: Sl 1, k2, m1, k2 tog, k1, m1, k1, k2 tog, p1, sl 1, k1, psso, (k1, m1) twice, k1, k2 tog, p1, sl 1, k1, psso, k1, m1, k3, m1, k2 tog, m2, k2 tog, m2, k2.

Row 4: K3, p1, k2, p1, k2, m1, k2 tog, p4, (k1, p3) twice, k1, p5, k1, m1, k2 tog, k1.

Row 5: Sl 1, k2, m1, k2 tog, k1, m1, k1, k2 tog, p1, sl 1, k1, psso, k1, p1, k1, k2 tog, p1, sl 1, k1, psso, k1, m1, k3, m1, k2 tog, k7.

Row 6: K9, m1, k2 tog, p4, (k1, p2) twice, k1, p5, k1, m1, k2 tog, k1.

Row 7: Sl 1, k2, m1, k2 tog, (k1, m1) twice, k2 tog, p1, sl 1, k1, psso, p1, k2 tog, p1, sl 1, psso, m1, k1, m1, k3, m1, k2 tog, (m2, k2 tog) 3 times, k1.

Row 8: K3, (p1, k2) 3 times, m1, k2 tog, p5, (k1, p1) twice, k1, p6, k1, m1, k2 tog, k1.

Row 9: Sl 1, k2, m1, k2 tog, k1, m1, k3, m1, sl 1, k2 tog, psso, p1, k3 tog, (m1, k3) twice, m1, k2 tog, k10.

Row 10: Cast off 6 sts, k5, m1, k2 tog, p7, k1, p8, k1, m1, k2 tog, k1.

Repeat rows 1–10 until length desired.

9: EILEEN

A beautiful dress in fine wool lace worn by Natalie Carbone, fifteen months, knitted by Eileen Kerney.
This dress fits children twelve to eighteen months old.

Materials

Approx. 5 balls 3-ply wool
Needles 3 mm (11) and 2.75 mm (12)
Length of ribbon for waist
4 small buttons
Tension 8½ sts to 2.5 cm (1″)

Front

** Using 3 mm (11) needles cast on 143 sts.
Knit 8 rows.
Continue in pattern thus:
Row 1: K4, * m1, sl 1, k1, psso, k5. Repeat from * ending with k4, instead of k5.
Row 2 and every alternate row: K1, purl to last st, k1.
Row 3: K2, * k2 tog, m1, k1, m1, sl 1, k1, psso, k2. Repeat from * ending with k3 instead of k2.
Row 5: K1, * k2 tog, m1, sl 1, k2 tog, psso, m1, sl 1, k1, psso. Repeat from * to last 2 sts, k2.
Row 7: K3, * m1, k1, m1, k4. Repeat from * to end of row.
Row 9: K1, * m1, sl 1, k1, psso, k5. Repeat from * to last 2 sts, m1, sl 1, k1, psso.
Row 11: K2, m1, sl 1, k1, psso, * k2, k2 tog, m1, k1, m1, sl 1, k1, psso. Repeat from * to last 6 sts, k2, k2 tog, m1, k2.
Row 13: K1, sl 1, k1, psso, * m1, sl 1, k1, psso, k2 tog, m1, sl 1, k2 tog, psso. Repeat from * to last 7 sts, m1, sl 1, k1, psso, k2 tog, m1, sl 1, k1, psso, k1.
Row 15: K2, m1, k4, * m1, k1, m1, k4. Repeat from * to last 2sts, m1, k2.
Row 16: K1, p to last st, k1.
Continue working pattern rows 1–16 until length desired, or approximately 29 cm (11½″).
Change to 2¾ mm (12) needles.
Next row: (K3 tog) twice, k2 tog until last 7 sts, k4 tog, k3 tog (69 sts).
Work in k1, p1, rib for 3 rows.

Work ribbon holes thus:
K1, (m1, k2 tog) to end of row, k1.
Work in k1, p1, rib for 3 rows **.

Change to 3 mm (11) needles.
Work 4 rows st, st ending with purl row.

Shape armholes:
Cast off 3 sts at beginning of next 2 rows then dec 1 st at both ends of next 2 rows (59 sts).
Commencing with row 9 of pattern, work until row 16, then work rows 1–16 of pattern.
Knit 1 row.
Purl 1 row.

Shape neck:
K21, cast off 17 sts, k21.
Continue on the last 21 sts, dec 1 st at neck edge on every row until 18 sts remain. Continue without shaping until armhole measures 9.5 cm (3¾″) on the straight.
Cast off.
Rejoin yarn at neck edge, work opposite side to correspond.

Back

Work as front **–**.
Change to 3 mm (11) needles, divide for back opening.
Next row: K31, turn. Cast on 7 sts for underlap. Leave remaining 38 sts on spare needle until required.
Next row: K7, p to end of row.
Work 2 rows st, st keeping 7 sts at centre back in garter st.

Shape armhole:
Cast off 3 sts from armhole edge at beginning of next row, then dec 1 st at armhole edge in next 2 rows (33 sts). Continue without shaping until armhole measures 9 cm (3½″) on the straight, ending at centre back.

Shape neck:
Cast off 13 sts. Work to end, dec 1 st at neck edge on next 2 rows.
Cast off.
Rejoin yarn at centre back, work to correspond with side already worked, keeping 7 sts in garter st for a border.
At centre back make a buttonhole when work measures 2 cm (¾″), then at intervals of 2.5 cm (1″) until you have made 4 buttonholes thus.
With right side facing k3, m2, k2 tog, work to end.
On the return row drop 1 loop of the m2 of the previous row, and k the other loop.

Sleeves (both alike)

Using 2.75 mm (12) needles cast on 42 sts.
K1, p1, rib for 2 rows.
Row 3: K1, (m1, k2 tog) to last st, k1.
Rows 4 and 5: K1, p1 rib.
Row 6: * P1, p twice in next st, p2, p twice in next st. Repeat from * to last 2sts, p1, p twice in next st (59 sts).
Change to 3 mm (11) needles.
Work rows 1–16 of lace pattern.

Shape sleeve top:
Work in st, st dec 1 st at both ends of every row until 19 sts remain.
Cast off, working k2 tog at each end of the casting-off row.

Continued on page 41

10: PIPPA

Two year old Annika Hellsing wearing a fine lace dress knitted by Eileen Kerney from a pattern dating from 1930.

Materials

Approx. 250 g 2-ply wool
Needles 3 mm (11)
6 small buttons
Length of cream ribbon to thread through the high waist

Measurements

Underarm 63.5 cm (25")
Neck to hem 53.5 cm (21")
Sleeve 5 cm (2")
Tension 8 sts to 2.5 cm (1") over st, st

Back

Cast on 143 sts.
Knit 7 rows.
Continue thus:
Row 1: K3, * k2 tog, m1, k1, m1, k2 tog tbl, k7. Repeat from * to last 8 sts, k2 tog, m1, k1, m1, k2 tog tbl, k3.
Row 2 and alternate rows: Purl.
Row 3: K2, * k2 tog, m1, k3, m1, k2 tog tbl, k5. Repeat from * to last 9 sts, k2 tog, m1, k3, m1, k2 tog tbl, k2.
Row 5: K1, * k2 tog, m1, k5, m1, k2 tog tbl, m1, sl 1, k2 tog, psso, m1. Repeat from * to last 10 sts, k2 tog, m1, k5, m1, k2 tog tbl, k1.
Row 7: K4, * m1, sl 1, k2 tog, psso, m1, k3. Repeat from * to last st, k1.
Row 8: Purl.
Continue in pattern until work measures 36 cm (14") or length desired, ending with Row 8.
Next row: K19, (k2 tog) 53 times, k18 (90 sts).
Work 3 rows in k1, p1, rib.
Next row: Work ribbon holes thus:
Rib 2, * rib 2 tog, m1, rib 2. Repeat from * to end of row.
Work 3 rows in k1, p1, rib.
Then work 2.5 cm (1") in st, st.

Shape armholes

Cast off 4 sts at beginning of next 2 rows. Dec 1 st each end of next 6 rows (70 sts). Continue until armholes measure 9 cm (3½").

Shape shoulders

Cast off 7 sts at beginning of next 4 rows and 8 sts on following 2 rows. Cast off remaining 26 sts.

Front

Work as back until armholes measure 6.5 cm (2½").

Shape neck:
K29, turn. Dec 1 st at neck edge of next 7 rows.
Continue until same length as back to shoulder.
Rejoin yarn to inner edge of remaining sts. Cast off centre 12 sts.
Work other side to correspond.

Sleeves

Cast on 47 sts.
Knit 7 rows, inc 12 sts evenly on last row (59 sts). Work 8 rows in skirt pattern. Continue in st, st until sleeve measures 4.5 cm (1¾").

Shape top:
Cast off 4 sts at beginning of next 2 rows. Dec 1 st at each end of next 6 rows then every alternate row until 24 sts on needle.
Cast off.

To make up

Join shoulder seam on each shoulder for 2.5 cm (1"). Work 1 row dc on shoulder and neck edge, then work row dc on shoulders, making 3 button loops on each front edge. Sew in sleeves. Join side and sleeve seams. Work row of 5 tr shells around neck, sleeves and hemline. Sew on six small buttons. Thread ribbon through holes at waist.
Press work lightly under damp cloth. A narrow knitted lace could be used around neck, sleeves and hemline if preferred.

To make up Eileen (page 39)

Join shoulder, side and sleeve seams. Sew in sleeves. Secure underlap at back waist.

Work evenly 1 row of single crochet around edges.
Work 2nd row of crochet thus: 3dc, make 3ch, work back into 3rd st to form picot.
Press seams and sew on buttons.

11: BONNETS

Four charming bonnets from nineteenth century patterns. Clockwise from lower left, Ruth Evelyn (this bonnet is from the christening set and the pattern appears on page 17), Lizzie, Tranquillity and Serenity. The materials required are listed with each pattern

LIZZIE

Bonnet adapted from an old pattern by Ruth Rintoule.

Materials

1 × 50 g ball DMC 10 cotton
Set of 4 needles 1.25 mm (18)
Small amount of embroidery thread in pink and green

Cast on 6 sts (2 sts on each of 3 needles). Work with 4th needle.
Round 1: (M1, k1) to end of round.
Round 2 and alternate rounds: Knit unless otherwise indicated.

Round 3: (M1, k2) to end of round.
Round 5: (M1, k3) to end of round.
Round 7: (M1, k4) to end of round.
Continue increasing in this manner, knitting an extra st between sections until there are 32 sts on each needle (96 sts).
Round 33: (M1, k1, m1, Sl 1, k1, psso, k13) to end of round.
Round 35: (M1, k3, m1, Sl 1, k1, psso, k12) to end of round.
Round 37: (M1, k5, m1, Sl 1, k1, psso, k11) to end of round.
Round 39: (M1, k7, m1, Sl 1, k1, psso, k10) to end of round.
Round 41: (M1, k9, m1, Sl 1, k1, psso, k9) to end of round.

Round 43: (M1, k11, m1, Sl 1, k1, psso, k8) to end of round.
Round 45: (M1, k13, m1, Sl 1, k1, psso, k7) to end of round.
Round 47: (M1, k15, m1, Sl 1, k1, psso, k6) to end of round.
Round 49: (M1, k17, m1, Sl 1, k1, psso, k5) to end of round.
Round 51: (M1, k19, m1, Sl 1, k1, psso, k4) to end of round.
Round 53: (M1, k21, m1, Sl 1, k1, psso, k3) to end of round.
Round 55: (M1, k23, m1, Sl 1, k1, psso, k2) to end of round.
Round 57: (M1, k25, m1, Sl 1, k1, psso, k1) to end of round.
Round 59: (M1, k27, m1, k2 tog) to end of round.
Knit 2 rounds.
Round 62: Knit across 2 needles. Cast off half of the sts on 3rd needle for back of neck.
Now work in rows.
Row 63: (K2 tog, m1) to end of row.
Row 64: Purl.
Row 65: As row 63.
Row 66: Purl.
Row 67: Knit.
Row 68: Purl.
Row 69: Knit.
Row 70: Purl.
Repeat rows 63–70, 5 times.
Next and following row: (K2, p2) to end of row.

Frill

Row 1: ** K2, (p1, m1, p1, k1, m1, k1). Repeat to last 2 sts, p2.
Row 2: (K2, p3, k3) to last 2 sts, p2.
Row 3: K2, (p1, m1, p1, m1, p1, k1, m1, k1, m1, k1). Repeat to last 2 sts, p2.
Row 4: K2, (p5, k5). Repeat to last 2 sts, p2.
Row 5: K2, (p1, m1, p3, m1, p1, k1, m1, k3, m1, k1). Repeat to last 2 sts, p2.
Row 6: K2, (p7, k7). Repeat to last 2 sts, p2 **
Cast off loosely.

Wrong side of work facing, pick up and purl 147 sts on last row of ribbed section.
Work 6 rows st, st.
Row 8: (K2 tog, m1) to last st, k1.
Row 9: Purl.
Row 10: As row 8.
Row 11: As row 9.
Work 8 rows st, st.
Cast off.

Back frill

With right side of work facing, pick up 108 sts around back of neck to start of other frill.
Row 1: (K2, p2) to end of row.
Work rows 1–6 of 1st frill **–**.
Cast off.
Turn under all edges. Slip stitch into place. Embroider rosebuds on front of bonnet. Attach ribbon ties.

TRANQUILLITY

An original nineteenth century design knitted by Barbara Hosking.

Materials

2×20 g balls DMC 20 cotton
2 sets 1.50 mm (16) needles (the second set is used to hold the sts in the ruched frill)

Back

Cast on 9 sts (3 sts on each of 3 needles).
Round 1 and every alternate round: Knit unless otherwise indicated. Place marker at end of round.
Round 2: (M1, k1), repeat to end of round.
Round 4: (M1, k2), repeat to end of round.
Round 6: (M1, k3), repeat to end of round.
Round 8: (M1, k4), repeat to end of round.
Round 10: (M1, k5), repeat to end of round.
Round 12: (M1, k6), repeat to end of round.
Round 14: (M1, k7), repeat to end of round.
Round 16: (M1, k8), repeat to end of round.
Round 18: (M1, k1, m1, k2 tog, k6), repeat to end of round.
Round 20: * M1, k1, (m1, k2 tog) twice, k5 *. Repeat from *–* to end of round.
Round 22: * M1, k1, (m1, k2 tog) 3 times, k4 *. Repeat from *–* to end of round.
Round 24: * M1, k1, (m1, k2 tog) 4 times, k3 *. Repeat from *–* to end of round.
Round 26: * M1, k1, (m1, k2 tog) 5 times, k2 *. Repeat from *–* to end of round.
Round 28: * M1, k1, (m1, k2 tog) 6 times, k1 *. Repeat from *–* to end of round.
Round 30: * M1, k1, (m1, k2 tog) 7 times *. Repeat from *–* to end of round.
Round 31: Knit.
Cast off.

Front

Cast on 53 sts.
Purl 1 row.

Row 1: Sl 1, k1, (m1, k2 tog) twice, k1, * m1, k1, sl 1, k1, psso, p1, k2 tog, k1, p1, k1, sl 1, k1, psso, p1, k2 tog, k1, m1, k2, (m1, k2 tog) twice, k1 *. Repeat from *–* to last 2 sts, k2.

Row 2: M1, k2 tog, p10, (k1, p2) twice, k1, p13, (k1, p2) twice, k1, p10.

Row 3: Sl 1, k2 tog, m1, k2 tog, m1, k2, * m1, k1, m1, sl 1, k1, psso, p1, k29, p1, sl 1, k1, psso, p1, k2 tog, (m1, k1) twice, k2 tog, m1, k2 tog, m1, k2 *. Repeat from *–* once, k2.

Row 4: M1, k2 tog, p11, (k1, p1) twice, k1, p15, k1, (p1, k1) twice, p11.

Row 5: Sl 1, k1, (m1, k2 tog) twice, k1, * m1, k3, m1, sl 1, k2 tog, psso, p1, k3 tog, m1, k3, m1, k2, (m1, k2 tog) twice, k1 *. Repeat from *–* once, k2.

Row 6: M1, k2 tog, p13, k1, p19, k1, p13.

Row 7: Sl 1, (k2 tog, m1) twice, k2, * m1, k5, m1, sl 1, k2 tog, psso, m1, k5, m1, k1, k2 tog, m1, k2 tog, m1, k2 *. Repeat from *–* once, k2.

Row 8: M1, k2 tog, p14, k1, p21, k1, p14.
Repeat rows 1–8, 21 times then work rows 1–7.
Cast off 31 sts purlwise, p7, k1, p14.

Row 1: Sl 1, k1, (m1, k2 tog) twice, k1, m1, k1, sl 1, k1, psso, p1, k2 tog, k1, p1, k1, sl 1, k1, psso, p1, k2 tog, k1, m1, k1.

Row 2: P4, k1, (p2, k1) twice, p10.

Row 3: Sl 1, (k2 tog, m1) twice, k2, m1, k1, m1, sl 1, k1, psso, p1, k2 tog, p1, sl 1, k1, psso, p1, k2 tog, (m1, k1) twice.

Row 4: P5, (k1, p1) twice, k1, p11.

Row 5: Sl 1, k1, (m1, k2 tog) twice, k1, m1, k3, m1, sl 1, k2 tog, psso, p1, k3 tog, m1, k3, m1, k1.

Row 6: P7, k1, p13.

Row 7: Sl 1, (k2 tog, m1) twice, k2, m1, k5, m1, sl 1, k2 tog, psso, m1, k5, m1, k1.

Row 8: P8, k1, p14.
Repeat rows 1–8, 3 times.
Cast off.
Join this piece to corresponding cast-on sts. Sew edge around bonnet back.

Base and first frill

With right side of bonnet facing and beginning in the centre of first rose leaf pattern, knit up 15 sts around the face, * pick up and knit 1 loop, m1, pick up and knit loop *. Repeat from *–* to end of front.
Knit up 15 sts around the other side to centre of first rose leaf (number of sts should be in multiples of 4).
Work 13 rows k2, p2, rib.

First frill ruching

Row 1: ** k2, * p1, m1, p1, k1, m1, k1 *. Repeat from *–* to last 2 sts, p2.

Row 2: K2, * p3, k3 *. Repeat from *–* to last 2 sts, p2.

Row 3: K2, * (p1, m1) twice, p1, k1, (m1, k1) twice *. Repeat from *–* to last 2 sts, p2.

Row 4: K2, * p5, k5 *. Repeat from *–* to last 2 sts, p2.

Row 5: K2, * p1, m1, p3, m1, p2, k1, m1, k3, m1, k1 *. Repeat from *–* to last 2 sts, p2.

Row 6: K2, * p7, k7 *. Repeat from *–* to last 2 sts, p2.
Cast off the k sts knitwise, p sts purlwise **.

Second frill ruching

Fold the ribbed base in half and pick up and knit 140 sts. Work **–** of frill ruching once.

Third frill ruching

Right side facing, pick up and knit 165 sts across first row of base piece and 111 sts across back and lower sides of bonnet.
Work **–** of first frill ruching once.
Cast off.

Ties (make 2)

Cast on 150 sts.
Knit 8 rows.
Cast off.

Rosettes (make 2)

Cast on 27 sts.
Work **–** of first frill ruching once.
Cast off in pattern.
Curve to form rosette. Stitch to ties. Attach the other end of ties to bonnet at end of ruching.

SERENITY

The original nineteenth century pattern has been amended and knitted by Ruth Rintoule.

Materials

2 balls DMC cotton 20
Needles 1.50 mm (16)
DMC embroidery thread: pink 818, green 772
Length of narrow pink ribbon

Main piece

Cast on 75 sts.

Row 1: Sl 1, k3, (m1, k2 tog) twice, m1, p2 tog, k2 tog, m2, k2 tog, m1, p2 tog, k2, k2 tog, m1, k1, m1, k2 tog, k2, m1, p2 tog, k2, m1, k2, Sl 1, k2 tog, psso, k2, m1, k1, m1, k2, Sl 1, k2 tog, psso, k2, m1, k2, m1, p2 tog, k2, k2 tog, m1, k1, m1, k2 tog, k2, m1, k1, m1, k2 tog, k2, m1, p2 tog, k2 tog, m2, k2 tog, m1, p2 tog, k1, m1, k2 tog, m1, k1, m1, p2 tog (m1, p2 tog) 3 times.

Row 2: M2, p2 tog (m1, p2 tog) twice, k5, m1, p2 tog, k2, p1, k1, m1, p2 tog, k3, p3, k3, m1, p2 tog, k3, p13, k3, m1, p2 tog, k3, p3, k3, m1, p2 tog, k2, p1, k1, m1, p2 tog, k8.

Row 3: Sl 1, k7, m1, p2 tog, k4, m1, p2 tog, k1, k2 tog, m1, k3, m1, k2 tog, k1, m1, p2 tog, k3, m1, k1, Sl 1, k2 tog, psso, k1, m1, k3, m1, k1, Sl 1, k2 tog, psso, k1, m1, k3, m1, p2 tog, k1, k2 tog, m1, k3, m1, k2 tog, k1, m1, p2 tog, k4, m1, p2 tog, k5 (m1, p2 tog) 3 times. Drop the last st.

Row 4: M2, p2 tog, (m1, p2 tog) twice, k5, m1, p2 tog, k4, m1, p2 tog, k2, p5, k2, m1, p2 tog, k4, p11, k4, m1, p2 tog, k2, p5, k2, m1, p2 tog, k4, m1, p2 tog, k8.

Row 5: Sl 1, k3, (m1, k2 tog) twice, m1, p2 tog, k2 tog, m2, k2 tog, m1, p2 tog, k2 tog, m1, k5, m1, k2 tog, m1, p2 tog, k4, m1, Sl 1, k2 tog, psso, m1, k5, m1, Sl 1, k2 tog, psso, m1, k4, m1, p2 tog, k2 tog, m1, k5, m1, k2 tog, m1, p2 tog, k2 tog, m2, k2 tog, m1, p2 tog, k1, m1, k2 tog, (k1, m1) twice, p2 tog, (m1, p2 tog) twice. Drop the last stitch.

Row 6: M2, p2 tog, (m1, p2 tog) twice, k6, m1, p2 tog, k2, p1, k1, m1, p2 tog, k1, p7, k1, m1, p2 tog, k5, p9, k5, m1, p2 tog, k1, p7, k1, m1, p2 tog, k2, p1, k1, m1, p2 tog, k8.

Row 7: Sl 1, k7, m1, p2 tog, k4, m1, p2 tog, k1, m1, k2, Sl 1, k2 tog, psso, k2, m1, k1, m1, p2 tog, k3, k2 tog, m1, k1, m1, k2, Sl 1, k2 tog, psso, k2, m1, k1, m1, k2 tog, k3, m1, p2 tog, k1, m1, k2, Sl 1, k2 tog, psso, k2, m1, k1, m1, p2 tog, k4, m1, p2 tog, k6, (m1, p2 tog) 3 times. Drop the last stitch.

Row 8: M2, p2 tog, (m1, p2 tog) twice, k6, m1, p2 tog, k4, m1, p2 tog, k2, p5, k2, m1, p2 tog, k4, p11, k4, m1, p2 tog, k2, p5, k2, m1, p2 tog, k4, m1, p2 tog, k8.

Row 9: Sl 1, k3, (m1, k2 tog) twice, m1, p2 tog, k2 tog, m2, k2 tog, m1, p2 tog, k2, m1, k1, Sl 1, k2 tog, psso, k1, m1, k2, m1, p2 tog, k2, k2 tog, m1, k3, m1, k1, Sl 1, k2 tog, psso, k1, m1, k3, m1, k2 tog, k2, m1, p2 tog, k2, m1, k1, Sl 1, k2 tog, psso, k1, m1, k2, m1, p2 tog, k2 tog, m2, k2 tog, m1, p2 tog, k1, m1, k2 tog, k2, m1, k1, (m1, p2 tog) 3 times. Drop the last stitch.

Row 10: M2, p2 tog, (m1, p2 tog) twice, k7, m1, p2 tog, k2, p1, k1, m1, p2 tog, k3, p3, k3, m1, p2 tog, k3, p13, k3, m1, p2 tog, k3, p3, k3, m1, p2 tog, k2, p1, k1, m1, p2 tog, k8.

Row 11: Sl 1, k7, m1, p2 tog, k4, m1, p2 tog, k3, m1, Sl 1, k2 tog, psso, m1, k3, m1, p2 tog, k1, k2 tog, m1, k5, m1, Sl 1, k2 tog, psso, m1, k5, m1, k2 tog, k1, m1, p2 tog, k3, m1, Sl 1, k2 tog, psso, m1, k3, m1, p2 tog, k4, m1, p2 tog, k7, (m1, p2 tog) 3 times. Drop the last stitch.

Row 12: Cast off 3 sts, k9, m1, p2 tog, k4, m1, p2 tog, k9, m1, p2 tog, k2, p15, k2, m1, p2 tog, k9, m1, p2 tog, k4, m1, p2 tog, k8.

Repeat rows 1–12 until there are 20 scallops on main piece of bonnet.

Crown

Cast on 11 sts.

Row 1: M1, k11.
Row 2: M1, k12.
Row 3: M1, k4, k2 tog, m1, k1, m1, k2 tog, k4.
Row 4: M1, k5, p3, k6.
Row 5: M1, k4, k2 tog, m1, k3, m1, k2 tog, k4.
Row 6: M1, k5, p5, k6.
Row 7: M1, k4, k2 tog, m1, k5, m1, k2 tog, k4.
Row 8: M1, k5, p7, k6.
Row 9: M1, k1, k2 tog, m1, k2, m1, k2 tog, m1, k1, sl 1, k2 tog, psso, k2, m1, k2 tog, m1, k1, m1, k2 tog, k1.
Row 10: M1, k2, p3, k2, p5, k2, p3, k3.
Row 11: M1, k1, k2 tog, m1, k3, m1, k2 tog, m1, k1, sl 1, k2 tog, psso, k1, m1, k2 tog, m1, k3, m1, k2 tog, k1.
Row 12: M1, k2, p5, k2, p3, k2, p5, k3.
Row 13: M1, k1, k2 tog, m1, k5, m1, k2 tog, m1, sl 1, k2 tog, psso, m1, k2 tog, m1, k5, m1, k2 tog, k1.
Row 14: M1, k2, p7, k5, p7, k3 (25 sts).
Row 15: Sl 1, k2, m1, k2, sl 1, k2 tog, psso, k2, m1, k2 tog, m1, k1, m1, k2 tog, m1, k2, sl 1, k2 tog, psso, k2, m1, k3.
Row 16: Sl 1, k3, p5, k2, p3, k2, p5, k4.
Row 17: Sl 1, k3, m1, k1, sl 1, k2 tog, psso, k1, m1, k2 tog, m1, k3, m1, k2 tog, m1, k1, sl 1, k2 tog, psso, k1, m1, k4.
Row 18: Sl 1, k4, p3, k2, p5, k2, p3, k5.
Row 19: Sl 1, k4, m1, sl 1, k2 tog, psso, m1, k2 tog, m1, k5, m1, k2 tog, m1, sl 1, k2 tog, psso, m1, k5.

Row 20: Sl 1, k8, p7, k9.

Row 21: Sl 1, k3, k2 tog, m1, k1, m1, k2 tog, m1, k2, sl 1, k2 tog, psso, k2, m1, k2 tog, m1, k1, m1, k2 tog, k4.

Row 22: Sl 1, k4, p3, k2, p5, k2, p3, k5.

Row 23: Sl 1, k2, k2 tog, m1, k3, m1, k2 tog, m1, k1, sl 1, k2 tog, psso, k1, m1, k2 tog, m1, k3, m1, k2 tog, k3.

Row 24: Sl 1, k3, p5, k2, p3, k2, p5, k4.

Row 25: Sl 1, k1, k2 tog, m1, k5, m1, k2 tog, m1, sl 1, k2 tog, psso, m1, k2 tog, m1, k5, m1, k2 tog, k2.

Row 26: Sl 1, k2, p7, k5, p7, k3.

Knit rows 15–26 twice, then decrease as follows:.

Row 1: Sl 1, k2, m1, k2, sl 1, k2 tog, psso, k2, m1, k2 tog, m1, k1, m1, k2 tog, m1, k2, sl 1, k2 tog, psso, k2, m1, k1, k2 tog.

Row 2: Sl 1, k2, p5, k2, p3, k2, p5, k2, k2 tog.

Row 3: Sl 1, k2, m1, k1, sl 1, k2 tog, psso, k1, m1, k2 tog, m1, k3, m1, k2 tog, m1, k1, sl 1, k2 tog, psso, k1, m1, k1, k2 tog.

Row 4: Sl 1, k2, p3, k2, p5, k2, p3, k2, k2 tog.

Row 5: Sl 1, k2, m1, sl 1, k2 tog, psso, m1, k2 tog, m1, k5, m1, k2 tog, m1, sl 1, k2 tog, psso, m1, k1, k2 tog.

Row 6: Sl 1, k5, p7, k5, k2 tog.

Row 7: Sl 1, k5, m1, k2, sl 1, k2 tog, psso, k2, m1, k4, k2 tog.

Row 8: Sl 1, k5, p5, k5, k2 tog.

Row 9: Sl 1, k5, m1, k1, sl 1, k2 tog, psso, k1, m1, k4, k2 tog.

Row 10: Sl 1, k5, p3, k5, k2 tog.

Row 11: Sl 1, k5, m1, sl 1, k2 tog, psso, k4, k2 tog.

Row 12: Sl 1, k10, k2 tog.

Row 13: Sl 1, k9, k2 tog.

Row 14: Sl 1, k8, k2 tog.

Row 15: Cast off.

Narrow lace edging

Cast on 11 sts.

Row 1: Sl 1, k1, m1, k2 tog, m1, k1, (m1, p2 tog) 3 times.

Row 2: M2, p2 tog, (m1, p2 tog) twice, k6.

Row 3: Sl 1, k5, (m1, p2 tog) 3 times. Drop the last stitch.

Row 4: As row 2.

Row 5: Sl 1, k1, m1, k2 tog, k1, m1, k1, (m1, p2 tog) 3 times. Drop the last stitch.

Row 6: M2, p2 tog, (m1, p2 tog) twice, k7.

Row 7: Sl 1, k6, (m1, p2 tog) 3 times. Drop the last stitch.

Row 8: As row 6.

Row 9: Sl 1, k1, m1, k2 tog, k2, m1, k1, (m1, p2 tog) 3 times. Drop the last stitch.

Row 10: M2, p2 tog, (m1, p2 tog) twice, k8.

Row 11: Sl 1, k7, (m1, p2 tog) 3 times. Drop the last stitch.

Row 12: Cast off 3 sts, k10.

Repeat rows 1–12 until there are 18 scallops on the lace.

To make up

Gently press bonnet pieces. Sew back of bonnet to front piece, easing fullness over the top to obtain correct shape. Sew the narrow lace across the neckline. Thread with narrow ribbon and trim with bullion stitch flowers and leaves if desired.

12: VICTORIAN COLLAR

Designed in the nineteenth century and expertly knitted by Dulcie Brewer, this collar would look delightful on a simple dress made in a plain dark colour in velvet, fine wool jersey or a heavy cotton.

Materials

5 × 20 g balls DMC 20 cotton
Needles 1.25 mm (18)
Tiny button and loop for fastening

The collar pattern has an edging of 12 sts each side of the centre lace. The instructions for the edgings have been edge row numbered for the sake of clarity. The line of asterisks ***** in the centre of the edgings indicate where the centre lace is worked in the pattern.
The rows 1-6 are your key to working the collar.

Edge

Row 1: (M1, k2 tog, k1, m1, p2 tog, k1, k3 tog, [k1, p1, k1 in next st] m1, p2 tog) ***** (m1, p2 tog, k1,

k3 tog, [k1, p1, k1 in next st] m1, p2 tog, k3).
Row 2: (M1, k2 tog, k1, m1, p2 tog, k2, m1, k2 tog, k1, m1, p2 tog) ***** (m1, p2 tog, k2, m1, k2 tog, k1, m1, p2 tog, k3).
Row 3: (M1, k2 tog, k1, m1, p2 tog, k5, m1, p2 tog) ***** (m1, p2 tog, k5, m1, p2 tog, k3).
Row 4: (M1, k2 tog, k1, m1, p2 tog, k1, k3 tog, [k1, p1, k1 in next st] m1, p2 tog) ***** (m1, p2 tog, k1, k3 tog, [k1, p1, k1 in next st] m1, p2 tog, k3.
Row 5: (M1, k2 tog, k1, m1, p2 tog, k2, m1, k2 tog, k1, m1, p2 tog) ***** (m1, p2 tog, k2, m1, k2 tog, k1, m1, p2 tog, k3).
Row 6: (M1, k2 tog, k1, m1, p2 tog, k5, m1, p2 tog) ***** (m1, p2 tog, k5, m1, p2 tog, k3).

Now that you have read and understood the edging row principle, proceed with one point of the collar.

Cast on 26 sts.

Row 1: Edge 1 (as row 1 of the key), k2, edge 1.

Row 2: Edge 2, k2, edge 2.

Row 3: Edge 3, k1, m1, k1, edge 3.

Row 4: Edge 4, k3, edge 4.

Row 5: Edge 5, k3, edge 5.

Row 6: Edge 6, k3, edge 6.

Row 7: Edge 1, k1, (m1, k1) twice, edge 1.

Row 8: Edge 2, k5, edge 2.

Row 9: Edge 3, k5, edge 3.

Row 10: Edge 4, k5, edge 4.

Row 11: Edge 5, k2, m1, k1, m1, k2, edge 5.

Row 12: Edge 6, k7, edge 6.

Row 13: Edge 1, k7, edge 1.

Row 14: Edge 2, k7, edge 2.

Row 15: Edge 3, k1, m1, k2 tog, m1, k1, m1, k2 tog, m1, k1, edge 3.

Row 16: Edge 4, k9, edge 4.

Row 17: Edge 5, k9, edge 5.

Row 18: Edge 6, k9, edge 6.

Row 19: Edge 1, k2, m1, k2 tog, m1, k1, m1, k2 tog, m1, k2, edge 1.

Row 20: Edge 2, k11, edge 2.

Row 21: Edge 3, k11, edge 3.

Row 22: Edge 4, k11, edge 4.

Row 23: Edge 5, k1, (m1, k2 tog) twice, m1, k1, (m1, k2 tog) twice, m1, k1, edge 5.

Row 24: Edge 6, k13, edge 6.

Row 25: Edge 1, k13, edge 1.

Row 26: Edge 2, k13, edge 2.

Row 27: Edge 3, k2, (m1, k2 tog) twice, m1, k1, (m1, k2 tog) twice, m1, k2, edge 3.

Row 28: Edge 4, k15, edge 4.

Row 29: Edge 5, k15, edge 5.

Row 30: Edge 6, k15, edge 6.

Row 31: Edge 1, k1, (m1, k2 tog) 3 times, m1, k1, (m1, k2 tog) 3 times, m1, k1, edge 1.

Row 32: Edge 2, k17, edge 2.

Row 33: Edge 3, k17, edge 3.

Row 34: Edge 4, k17, edge 4.

Row 35: Edge 5, k2, (m1, k2 tog) 3 times, m1, k1, (m1, k2 tog) 3 times, m1, k2, edge 5.

Row 36: Edge 6, k19, edge 6.

Row 37: Edge 1, k19, edge 1.

Row 38: Edge 2, k19, edge 2.

Row 39: Edge 3, k1, (m1, k2 tog) 4 times, m1, k1, (m1, k2 tog) 4 times, m1, k1, edge 3.

Row 40: Edge 4, k21, edge 4.

Row 41: Edge 5, k21, edge 5.

Row 42: Edge 6, k21, edge 6.

Row 43: Edge 1, k2, (m1, k2 tog) 4 times, m1, k1, (m1, k2 tog) 4 times, m1, k2, edge 1.

Row 44: Edge 2, k23, edge 2.

Row 45: Edge 3, k23, edge 3.

Row 46: Edge 4, k23, edge 4.

Row 47: Edge 5, k1, (m1, k2 tog) 4 times, m1, k2, m2, k2 tog, k1, (m1, k2 tog) 4 times, m1, k1, edge 5.

Row 48: Edge 6, k13, p1, k12, edge 6.

Row 49: Edge 1, k9, k2 tog, m2, (k2 tog) twice, m2, k2 tog, k9, edge 1.

Row 50: Edge 2, k11, p1, k3, p1, k10, edge 2.

Row 51: Edge 3, k2, (m1, k2 tog) twice, m1, k1, (k2 tog, m2, k2 tog) 3 times, k1, (m1, k2 tog) twice, m1, k2, edge 3.

Row 52: Edge 4, k10, (p1, k3) twice, p1, k9, edge 4.

Row 53: Edge 5, k6, (k2 tog, m2, k2 tog) 4 times, k6, edge 5.

Row 54: Edge 6, k8, p1, (k3, p1) 3 times, k7, edge 6.

Row 55: Edge 1, k1, m1, k2 tog, m1, k1, (k2 tog, m2, k2 tog) 5 times, k1, m1, k2 tog, m1, k1, edge 1.

Row 56: Edge 2, k7, p1, (k3, p1) 4 times, k6, edge 2.

Row 57: Edge 3, k3, (k2 tog, m2, k2 tog) 6 times, k3, edge 3.

Row 58: Edge 4, k5, p1, (k3, p1) 5 times, k4, edge 4.

Row 59: Edge 5, k1, m1, (k2 tog, m2, k2 tog) 7 times, m1, k1, edge 5.

Row 60: Edge 6, k4, p1, (k3, p1) 6 times, k3, edge 6.

Row 61: Edge 1, (k2 tog, m2, k2 tog) 8 times, edge 1.

Row 62: Edge 2, k2, p1, (k3, p1) 7 times, k1, edge 2.

Row 63: Edge 3, m1, p1, k1, (k2 tog, m2, k2 tog) 7 times, k1, m1, p1, edge 3.

Row 64: Edge 4, m1, p2 tog, (k3, p1) 7 times, k2, p1, p2 tog, edge 4.

Row 65: Edge 5, m1, p2 tog, m1, p1, k2, (k2 tog, m2, k2 tog) 6 times, k2, m1, p1, m1, p2 tog, edge 5.

Row 66: Edge 6, (m1, p2 tog) twice, k4, p1, (k3, p1) 5 times, k3, (m1, p2 tog) twice, edge 6.

Row 67: Edge 1, (m1, p2 tog) 3 times, m1, p1, k1, (k2 tog, m2, k2 tog) 5 times, k1, m1, p1, (m1, p2 tog) 3 times, edge 1.

Row 68: Edge 2, (m1, p2 tog) 4 times, (k3, p1) 5 times, k2, (m1, p2 tog) 4 times, edge 2.

Row 69: Edge 3, (m1, p2 tog) 4 times, m1, p1, k2, (k2 tog, m2, k2 tog) 4 times, k2, m1, p1, (m1, p2 tog) 4 times, edge 3.

Row 70: Edge 4, (m1, p2 tog) 5 times, k4, p1, (k3, p1) 3 times, k3, (m1, p2 tog) 5 times, edge 4.

Row 71: Edge 5, (m1, p2 tog) 6 times, m1, p1, k1, (k2 tog, m2, k2 tog) 3 times, k1, m1, p1, (m1, p2 tog) 6 times, edge 5.

Row 72: Edge 6, (m1, p2 tog) 7 times, (k3, p1) 3 times, k2, (m1, p2 tog) 7 times, edge 6.

Row 73: Edge 1, (m1, p2 tog) 7 times, m1, p1, k2, (k2 tog, m2, k2 tog) twice, k2, m1, p1, (m1, p2 tog) 7 times, edge 1.

Row 74: Edge 2, (m1, p2 tog) 8 times, k4, (p1, k3) twice, (m1, p2 tog) 8 times, edge 2.

Row 75: Edge 3, (m1, p2 tog) 9 times, m1, p1, k1, (k2 tog, m2, k2 tog), k1, m1, p1, (m1, p2 tog) 9 times, edge 3.

The edge as worked from the key is now discontinued. These sts are henceforth knit, as the point is decreased, as follows:

Row 1: M1, (k2 tog) twice, k6, (m1, p2 tog) 12 times, k1, p1, (m1, p2 tog) 12 times, k10.
Row 2: M1, (k2 tog) twice, k6, (m1, p2 tog) 25 times, k9.
Row 3: M1, (k2 tog) twice, k5, (m1, p2 tog) 25 times, k9.
Row 4: M1, (k2 tog) twice, k5, (m1, p2 tog) 25 times, k8.
Row 5: M1, (k2 tog) twice, k4, (m1, p2 tog) 25 times, k8.
Row 6: M1, (k2 tog) twice, k4, (m1, p2 tog) 25 times, k7.
Row 7: M1, (k2 tog) twice, k3, (m1, p2 tog) 25 times, k7.
Row 8: M1, (k2 tog) twice, k3, (m1, p2 tog) 25 times, k6.
Row 9: M1, (k2 tog) twice, k2, (m1, p2 tog) 25 times, k6.
Row 10: M1, (k2 tog) twice, k2, (m1, p2 tog) 25 times, k5.
Row 11: M1, (k2 tog) twice, k1, (m1, p2 tog) 25 times, k5.
Row 12: M1, (k2 tog) twice, k1, (m1, p2 tog) 25 times, k4.
Row 13: M1, (k2 tog) twice, (m1, p2 tog) 25 times, k4.
Row 14: M1, (k2 tog) twice, (m1, p2 tog) 25 times, k3.
Row 15: M1, (k2 tog) twice, k1, (m1, p2 tog) 24 times, k3.
Row 16: M1, (k2 tog) twice, k1, (m1, p2 tog) 23 times, k4.
Row 17: M1, (k2 tog) twice, (m1, p2 tog) 23 times, k4.
Row 18: M1, (k2 tog) twice, (m1, p2 tog) 23 times, k3.
Row 19: M1, (k2 tog) twice, k1, (m1, p2 tog) 22 times, k3.
Row 20: M1, (k2 tog) twice, k1, (m1, p2 tog) 21 times, k4.
Row 21: M1, (k2 tog) twice, (m1, p2 tog) 21 times, k4.
Row 22: M1, (k2 tog) twice, (m1, p2 tog) 21 times, k3.
Row 23: M1, (k2 tog) twice, k1, (m1, p2 tog) 20 times, k3.
Row 24: M1, (k2 tog) twice, k1, (m1, p2 tog) 19 times, k4.
Row 25: M1, (k2 tog) twice, (m1, p2 tog) 19 times, k4.
Row 26: M1, (k2 tog) twice, (m1, p2 tog) 19 times, k3.
Row 27: M1, (k2 tog) twice, k1, (m1, p2 tog) 18 times, k3.
Row 28: M1, (k2 tog) twice, k1, (m1, p2 tog) 17 times, k4.
Row 29: M1, (k2 tog) twice, (m1, p2 tog) 17 times, k4.
Row 30: M1, (k2 tog) twice, (m1, p2 tog) 17 times, k3.
Row 31: M1, (k2 tog) twice, k1, (m1, p2 tog) 16 times, k3.
Row 32: M1, (k2 tog) twice, k1, (m1, p2 tog) 15 times, k4.
Row 33: M1, (k2 tog) twice, (m1, p2 tog) 15 times, k4.
Row 34: M1, (k2 tog) twice, (m1, p2 tog) 15 times, k3.
Row 35: M1, (k2 tog) twice, k1, (m1, p2 tog) 14 times, k3.
Row 36: M1, (k2 tog) twice, k1, (m1, p2 tog) 13 times, k4.
Row 37: M1, (k2 tog) twice, (m1, p2 tog) 13 times, k4.
Row 38: M1, (k2 tog) twice, (m1, p2 tog) 13 times, k3.
Row 39: M1, (k2 tog) twice, k1, (m1, p2 tog) 12 times, k3.
Row 40: M1, (k2 tog) twice, k1, (m1, p2 tog) 11 times, k4.
Row 41: M1, (k2 tog) twice, (m1, p2 tog) 11 times, k4.
Row 42: M1, (k2 tog) twice, (m1, p2 tog) 11 times, k3.

Row 43: M1, (k2 tog) twice, k1, (m1, p2 tog) 10 times, k3.
Row 44: M1, (k2 tog) twice, k1, (m1, p2 tog) 9 times, k4.
Row 45: M1, (k2 tog) twice, (m1, p2 tog) 9 times, k4.
Row 46: M1, (k2 tog) twice, (m1, p2 tog) 9 times, k3.
Row 47: M1, (k2 tog) twice, k1, (m1, p2 tog) 8 times, k3.
Row 48: M1, (k2 tog) twice, k1, (m1, p2 tog) 7 times, k3.
Row 49: M1, (k2 tog) twice, (m1, p2 tog) 7 times, k4.
Row 50: M1, (k2 tog) twice, (m1, p2 tog) 7 times, k3.
Row 51: M1, (k2 tog) twice, k1, (m1, p2 tog) 6 times, k3.
Row 52: M1, (k2 tog) twice, k1, (m1, p2 tog) 5 times, k4.
Row 53: M1, (k2 tog) twice, (m1, p2 tog) 5 times, k4.
Row 54: M1, (k2 tog) twice, (m1, p2 tog) 5 times, k3.
Row 55: M1, (k2 tog) twice, k1, (m1, p2 tog) 4 times, k3.
Row 56: M1, (k2 tog) twice, k1, (m1, p2 tog) 3 times, k4.
Row 57: M1, (k2 tog) twice, (m1, p2 tog) 3 times, k4.
Row 58: M1, (k2 tog) twice, (m1, p2 tog) 3 times, k3.
Row 59: M1, (k2 tog) twice, k1, (m1, p2 tog) twice, k3.
Row 60: M1, (k2 tog) twice, k1, m1, p2 tog, k4.
Row 61: M1, (k2 tog) twice, m1, p2 tog, k4.
Row 62: M1, (k2 tog) twice, m1, p2 tog, k3.
Row 63: M1, (k2 tog) twice, k4.
Row 64: M1, (k2 tog) twice, k3.
Row 65: M1, (k2 tog) 3 times.
Row 66: M1, (k2 tog) twice.
Row 67: Sl 1, k2 tog, psso.
Cut thread. Fasten off at point.

Knit 4 more of these points. Join together by herringbone edge, or lace with a thread or fine ribbon, leaving ends at lower edge to form points. Extra points could be added if desired.

Lace for neck

Cast on 4 sts.
Row 1: Sl 1, k1, m1, k2.
Row 2: K5.
Row 3: Sl 1, k2, m1, k2.
Row 4: K6.
Row 5: Sl 1, k1, m2, k2 tog, m1, k2.
Row 6: K5, p1, k2.
Row 7: Sl 1, k5, m1, k2.
Row 8: Cast off 5 sts, k3.
Repeat rows 1–8 until length required to edge neckline. Cast off. Stitch lace to neckline. Lightly press collar. Fasten at neck with a button and loop.

13: CANTERBURY LACE

A delicate collar knitted by Edna Lomas is modelled by Alice Rose Cottee. Alice is holding an early Rupert monster book by Mary Tourtel. In the background you will see the drawing instruments used by Mary Tourtel to create Rupert Bear. The artist was Alice's great-great-great aunt Mary, information of special interest to arctophiles.

Materials

1 × 50 g ball DMC Cebelia 20
Needles 2 mm (14)
Length of ribbon

Cast on 27 sts.
Row 1: Sl 1, k13, m1, k2, m1, (k2 tog) twice, m1, k2 tog, m1, k2, m2, k2 tog, k1.
Row 2: K3, p1, k2, p20. Turn, leaving 3 sts on needle.
Row 3: K12, m1, k2 tog, k1, k2 tog, m1, k1, m1, k2 tog, m1, k6.
Row 4: K6, p21. Turn, leaving 3 sts on needle.
Row 5: K11, m1, k2 tog, m1, sl 1, k2 tog, psso, m1, k3, m1, k2 tog, m1, k2, m2, k2 tog, m2, k2.
Row 6: K3, (p1, k2) twice, p22, k3.
Row 7: Sl 1, k2, p12, m1, k2 tog, m1, (k2 tog) twice, m1, k2, m1, k2 tog, m1, k9.
Row 8: Cast off 4 sts, k4 (not counting sts on needle after cast off) p11, k12. Turn, leaving 3 sts on needle.
Row 9: P11, (m1, k2 tog) 3 times, k1, k2 tog, m1, k1, m1, k2 tog, m1, k2, m2, k2 tog, k1.
Row 10: K3, p1, k2, p13, k11. Turn.
Row 11: P12, (m1, k2 tog) twice, m1, sl 1, k2 tog, psso, m1, k3, m1, k2 tog, m1, k6.

Row 12: K6, p13, k15.
Row 13: Sl 1, k12, k2 tog, (m1, k2 tog) 3 times, k2 tog, m1, k2, (m1, k2 tog) twice, k1, m2, k2 tog, m2, k2.
Row 14: K3, (p1, k2) twice, p24. Turn.
Row 15: K10, k2 tog, k1, m1, k2 tog, m1, k1, m1, k2 tog, k1, k2 tog, (m1, k2 tog) twice, k3.
Row 16: Cast off 4 sts, k4, p23. Turn.
Row 17: K10, (k2 tog, m1) twice, k3, m1, sl 1, k2 tog, psso, (m1, k2 tog) twice, k1, m2, k2 tog, k1.
Row 18: K3, p1, k2, p22, k3.
Row 19: Sl 1, k2, p9, p2 tog, m1, k2 tog, m1, k2, m1, (k2 tog) twice, (m1, k2 tog) twice, k5.
Row 20: K6, p11, k10. Turn.
Row 21: P10, p2 tog, m1, k1, m1, k2 tog, k1, k2 tog, (m1, k2 tog) twice, k1, m2, k2 tog, m2, k2.
Row 22: K3, p1, k2, p1, k2, p9, k11. Turn.
Row 23: P9, p2 tog, m1, k3, m1, sl 1, k2 tog, psso, (m1, k2 tog) twice, k8.
Row 24: Cast off 4 sts, k4, p9, k13.
Repeat rows 1–24, 20 times.
Cast off.
Thread ribbon through holes at neck edge.
Tie at front.

14: SIREN

Siren, a basic all-in-one garment, is worn by Annalise O'Toole aged fifteen weeks. The suit has been enhanced by the addition of knitted lace edgings stitched to the turned back moss stitch cuffs. A length of Siren Lace forms the collar. Care needs to be taken with collars on baby clothes — make sure the ribbons are not too long and are secure. Eileen Kerney knitted this useful garment, designed for a baby three to six months old. (No date on handwritten instructions — c. late 1930s.) Annalise is wearing Shoes from Bears on page 61. Patchwork quilt by Joan Jackson.

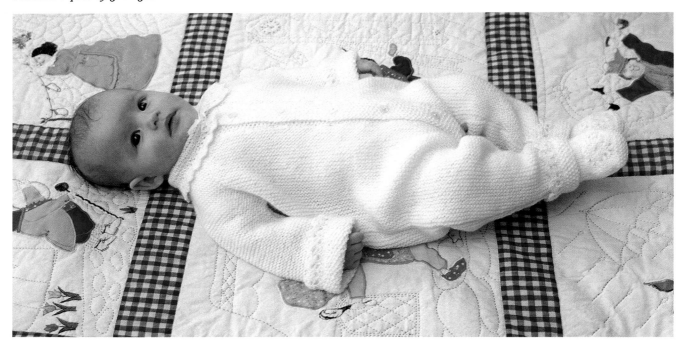

Materials

5 balls 3-ply baby wool
Needles 3 mm (11)
6 buttons
5 lengths Siren Lace
Needles 2 mm (14)

Measurements

Underarm 52 cm (20½″)
Tension 12 sts to 2.5 cm (1″) over garter st

SUIT

Back

Cast on 55 sts.
Knit 1 row.
Mark end of row for leg, the other end for yoke edge.
Work in garter st. At leg end cast on 6 sts once and 5 sts 4 times. Whilst at yoke edge, cast on 4 sts twice and 3 sts 6 times (107 sts). Continue in garter st until work measures 4.5 cm (1¾″) from beginning. At yoke inc 1 st in next row and every 4th row 3 times, then alternate rows 4 times (115 sts). Work until back measures 11 cm (5¼″).

Continue in garter st. From leg end cast off 5 sts 4 times, 6 sts once, 13 sts once (76 sts). Continue until back measures 17 cm (6¾″) from beginning. At leg end cast on 13 sts once, 6 sts once, 5 sts 4 times (115 sts).

Continue until back measures 22cm (8¾″) from beginning. Continue in garter st. At yoke edge dec 1 st in alternate rows 4 times, then every 4th row 4 times (107 sts). When work measures 27 cm (10¾″) from beginning, at yoke edge cast off 3 sts 6 times, 4 sts twice. At the same time, when work measures 28cm, cast off at leg end 5 sts 4 times, 6 sts once (55 sts).

Cast off.

Right front

Beginning at front edge, cast on 76 sts.
Knit 5 rows. Mark end of row for leg end. At leg cast on 13 sts once, 6 sts once, 5 sts 4 times (115 sts). Work in garter st until right front measures 6 cm (2¼"). At yoke edge dec 1 st in alternate rows 4 times, then every 4th row 4 times (107 sts). Continue until work measures 11 cm (4¼"). Cast off 3 sts at yoke edge 6 times, 4 sts twice. When work measures 12 cm (4¾") from leg end cast off 5 sts 4 times, 6 sts once (55 sts).
Cast off.

Left front

Cast on 76 sts.
Knit 5 rows.
Mark beginning of last row for leg end. Work as for right front, reversing shaping.

Sleeves and yoke

Sleeves and yoke are worked in one piece from right to left cuff.
Cast on 48 sts.
Work in moss st for 3 cm (1¼"). Change to garter st until work measures 13 cm (5¼") from cuff. Mark each end of needle for beginning of yoke. Work in garter st for 1.5 cm (½"). Dec 1 st each end of next row, then every 4th row once, then every 6th row 3 times (38 sts). Continue in garter st until work measures 7.5 cm (3") from markers.

Divide for neck:
K19, sl sts to holder. K to end of row. Continue on the 19 sts for back yoke until 9.5 cm (3¾") from dividing row. End at neck edge. Sl sts to holder. Sl sts from first holder to needle for right front yoke, continue in garter st. At neck edge cast off 3 sts once, 2 sts twice. Dec 1 st alternate rows twice, then every 4th row twice (8 sts). Mark the last row when work measures 4 cm (1½") above dividing row. Cast off. Cast on 8 sts for left front yoke. Work as for right front from marker to cast-off. Remove marker. At neck inc 1 st in next row, then every 4th row once, every alternate row twice. Cast on 2 sts twice, 3 sts once (19 sts). Sl sts from holder to needle. Knit across all sts (38 sts). Continue until work measures 19 cm (7½") above yoke marker.
Place marker at each end for end of yoke. Knit until 12.75 cm (5") from last marker. Moss st for 3 cm (1¼").
Cast off.

Neck border

Beginning at right front, pick up and knit 49 sts around neck edge.
Moss st for 1.5 cm (½").
Cast off.
Sew back and fronts to yoke. Sew side and sleeve seams, taking care to sew moss st cuff seams on right side of cuff.

Leg borders (make 2)

Cast on 8 sts.
Work in moss st for 18 cm (7").
Cast off.
Stitch to ends of legs to form turn-ups.

Front borders

Cast on 8 sts.
Work in moss st for 31 cm (12¼").
Cast off.
Work another border with buttonholes: Cast on 8 sts. Work in moss st for 31 cm (12¼") making 6 buttonholes thus: k4, m1, k2 tog, k2, the first 4 cm from the bottom and the 6th 1.5 cm (½") from the top.
Cast off.
Sew borders to front, taking care to overlap the button bands.
Sew on buttons.

Reverse bands for boy.

LACE

Cast on 20 sts.
Row 1: Sl 1, k1, k2 tog, m1, k3, m1, k2 tog, k1, m1, k2 tog, k1, m2, k2 tog, k5.
Row 2: K7, p1, k6, m1, k2 tog, k5.
Row 3: Sl 1, k1, k2 tog, m1, k3, m1, k2 tog, k1, m1, k2 tog, k9.
Row 4: K14, m1, k2 tog, k5.
Row 5: Sl 1, k1, k2 tog, m1, k3, m1, k2 tog, k1, m1, k2 tog, k1, m2, k2 tog, m2, k6.
Row 6: K7, p1, k2, p1, k6, m1, k2 tog, k5.
Row 7: Sl 1, k1, k2 tog, m1, k3, m1, k2 tog, k1, m1, k2 tog, k12.
Row 8: Cast off 4 sts, k12, m1, k2 tog, k5.
Repeat rows 1–8 until length desired.

15: ANNALISE

Another practical all-in-one garment, worn by Annalise O'Toole. The st, st suit, with narrow lace cuffs and detachable collar in Daisy Lace, was knitted by Eileen Kerney. Omit lace trims to make this suit appropriate for a boy.
Patchwork quilt by Joan Jackson.

Materials

4 balls 3-ply baby wool
Needles 2.75 mm (12)
2 lengths Narrow Daisy Lace for cuffs
1 length Daisy Lace for collar

Measurements

Suitable for 3 to 6 months
Tension 8 sts to 2.5 cm (1") over st, st

Sleeves and yoke

Cast on 54 sts.
Work in st, st for 13 cm (5¼").
Place marker each end of row.
Work until 14 cm (5½") ending with purl row.

Shape armholes:
Cast off 2 sts at beginning of next 2 rows.
Dec 1 st at beginning of next 14 rows (36 sts).
Work until 21 cm (8¼") from beginning, ending with purl row.
Divide work in two equal parts; k18 from right edge, sl sts onto st holder. Continue on 18 sts from right edge, sl sts onto st holder.
Continue on 18 sts from left edge.
Work until 25 cm (10") from beginning.
Cast off.

Cast on 18 sts, work in st, st for 18 rows.
Sl these 18 sts onto st holder.
Place 18 sts from right edge holder onto needle and shape front neck.
At neck edge, on alternate rows cast off 3 sts once, 2 sts once, dec 1 st alternate rows, 4 times.
Work until 26 cm (10¼") from beginning.

Inc at neck edge only as follows:
Inc 1 st on next row, then alternate rows 3 times. Cast on 2 sts once, cast on 3 sts once (18 sts). Continue on these 18 sts and the 18 sts from holder and join together (36 sts).
Work until 32 cm (12½") from beginning. Inc 1 st at beginning of next 14 rows. Cast on 2 sts at beginning of next 2 rows (54 sts). Work until 37 cm (14½") from beginning. Place marker at each end.
Work until 50 cm (20") from beginning.
Cast off.

Front

Cast on 24 sts (for half of leg). Work in st, st.
Inc 1 st each end of every 4th row 4 times and every 6th row 4 times (40).
Work until front measures 15 cm (6") from beginning. Sl sts onto holder.
Knit second half of leg to correspond.

To join legs:
Work 40 sts, cast on 12 sts, knit 40 sts of other leg (92 sts). Continue until work measures 28 cm (11") from beginning, ending with purl row. Dec 1 st each end of every 4th row 10 times (72 sts). Continue until work measures 39 cm (15¼").

Shape armholes:
Cast off 3 sts at beginning of next 2 rows. Cast off 2 sts at beginning of next 12 rows (42 sts).

Half back

Cast on 24 sts.
Work as for front until half back measures 15 cm (6") from beginning. Cast on 7 sts at right edge (47 sts).
Work until 20 cm (7¾") from beginning. Now work in short rows as follows:
Start at right edge, work to last 5 sts, turn, work back.
Work to within last 10 sts, turn, work back.
Work to within last 15 sts, turn, work back.
Work to within last 20 sts, turn, work back.
Work to within last 25 sts, turn, work back.
Work to within last 30 sts, turn, work back.
Work on all sts.
Continue until work measures 31 cm (12¼"). Dec 1 st at left edge every 4th row 10 times (37 sts).
Continue until back measures 42 cm (16½").

Shape armhole:
At left edge cast off 3 sts once, 2 sts alternate rows 6 times (22 sts).
Cast off.

Work second half of back to correspond, reversing all shapings.

To make up

Press the work. Sew side and sleeve seams. Attach yoke to body. Sew armholes.

Attached bootee

Pick up and knit 48 sts around bottom of leg.
Work in st, st dec 1 st both ends of next row (46 sts).
Eyelets: K3, * k2 tog, m1, k2. Repeat from * ending last repeat m1, k1.
Continue in st, st dec 6 sts evenly across row (40 sts).
Work 7 rows:
Slip first 4 sts from leg seam onto st holder, work next 12 sts for top of foot, place remaining 24 sts on holder.
Work on 12 sts for 15 rows, place 12 sts on holder.
Join yarn, work 24 sts from holder.
Pick up and knit 10 sts along side edge of top, k4 from holder (60 sts).
Work 6 rows.
Cast off 14 sts on one side and 34 sts on other side (12 sts).
Work for 7 cm.
Cast off.

To make up

Sew leg and sole seams.
Make a knitted cord. Thread through eyelet holes for ties.
Sew back seam. Sew in zip fastener with tiny sts or make a buttonhole band as for Siren on page 53.
Sew on Daisy Lace at collar and Narrow Daisy Lace at cuffs.

DAISY LACE

Cast on 20 sts.
Row 1: Sl 1, k2, (m1, k2 tog) twice, k4, (m1, k2 tog) twice, k5.
Row 2: Sl 1, k4, p6, m1, k2 tog, k7.
Row 3: Sl 1, k2, (m1, k2 tog) twice, k2, (k2 tog, m1) twice, k3, m2, k2 tog, m2, k2.
Row 4: Sl 1, k2, m1, k2 tog, k1, m1, k2 tog, k1, p7, k7.
Row 5: Sl 1, k2, (m1, k2 tog) twice, k1, (k2 tog, m1) twice, k11.
Row 6: Sl 1, k1, m2, k2 tog, k1, k2 tog, m2, k2 tog, k1, p6, k7.
Row 7: Sl 1, k2, (m1, k2 tog) twice, (k2 tog, m1) twice, k5, m1, k2 tog, k3, m1, k2 tog, k1.
Row 8: Sl 1, k11, p5, k7.

Row 9: Sl 1, k2, (m1, k2 tog) twice, k2, (m1, k2 tog) twice, k2, k2 tog, m2, sl 1, k2 tog, psso, m2, (k2 tog) twice.
Row 10: Sl 1, k2, m1, k2 tog, k1, m1, k2 tog, k2, p6, k7.
Row 11: Sl 1, k2, (m1, k2 tog) twice, k3, (m1, k2 tog) twice, k9.
Row 12: Cast off 3 sts, k5, p7, k7.
Repeat rows 1–12 until length desired.

NARROW DAISY LACE

Cast on 12 sts.
Knit 1 row.
Row 1: Sl 1, k2 tog, m1, k2, m1, k2 tog, k1, m2, k2 tog, m2, k2.
Row 2: Sl 1, (k2, p1) twice, k8.
Row 3: Sl 1, k2 tog, m1, k2, m1, k2 tog, k8.
Row 4: Sl 1, k14.
Row 5: Sl 1, k2 tog, m1, k2, m1, k2 tog, k1, (m2, k2 tog) 3 times, k1.
Row 6: Sl 1, (k2, p1) 3 times, k8.
Row 7: Sl 1, k2 tog, m1, k2, m1, k2 tog, k11.
Row 8: Sl 1, k2 tog, k15.
Row 9: Sl 1, k2 tog, m1, k2, m1, k2 tog, k4, (m2, k2 tog) twice, k2 tog.
Row 10: Sl 1, (k2, p1) twice, k11.
Row 11: Sl 1, k2 tog, m1, k2, m1, k2 tog, k11.
Row 12: Cast off 6 sts, k11.
Repeat rows 1–12 until length desired.

16: BEARS

A collection of handcrafted bears by Kathie Savage (see Suppliers, page 119) wearing knitted vests and selecting footwear. The garments are suitable for a six months old child. Knitted by Eileen Kerney. The vests clockwise from top left are Jasper, Oliver and Merric. The knitted footwear, from the top, are High Boots, Battenberg and Shoes.

Materials

1 ball 3-ply baby wool for each pair of boots and shoes
Needles 2.75 mm (12) and 3 mm (11)
2 balls 3-ply baby wool for each vest
Needles 3.25 mm (10)

OLIVER

Cast on 79 sts.
**Row 1: * K2, p2. Repeat from * to last 3 sts, k3.
Row 2: K1, p1, * k2, p2. Repeat from * to last st, k1 **.
Work in pattern as given from **–** until work measures 19 cm (7½") from commencement. End with right side facing for next row.

Shape armholes
Row 1: Cast off 4 sts. Pattern to end of row.
Row 2: Cast off 4 sts. Pattern to end of row.
Row 3: Work in rib pattern.
Row 4: Work in rib pattern.
Repeat rows 3 and 4 until work measures 23 cm (9").
End with right side facing for next row.

Shape neck:
Row 1: Pattern 19 sts. Continue on these sts thus:
Row 2: Work in pattern.
Row 3: Work in pattern.
Repeat rib pattern rows until work measures 26 cm (10¼"), ending with 2nd row of rib pattern.
Cast off. Cut yarn and join at neck edge. Work on remaining sts to correspond with other side.

Back

Work as for front

To make up

Press lightly. Sew up side and shoulder seams.
With right side facing and commencing at left shoulder seam, work 1 round of 1 tr, 1 ch evenly around neck edge. Work a picot edge around armholes as well. Thread knitted cord through holes at neck.

JASPER

Cast on 62 sts.
Row 1: Knit.
Row 2: Purl.
Row 3: Knit.

Row 4: Sl 1, k2, k2 tog, k1, * (m1, k1) twice, (k2 tog) twice, k1. Repeat from * 6 times, (m1, k1) twice, k2 tog, k3.
Row 5: Purl.
Repeat rows 4 and 5.
Row 8: As row 4.
Row 9: Knit.
Row 10: Purl.
Row 11: K2 tog, knit to last 2 sts, k2 tog (60 sts).
Row 12: Sl 1, k1, k2 tog, k1, * (m1, k1) twice, (k2 tog) twice, k1. Repeat from * 6 times, m1, k1, m1, k2 tog, k2.
Row 13: Purl.
Repeat rows 12 and 13.
Continue thus:
Work 3 rows, (k6, p6) to end of row, then work 3 rows, (p6, k6) to end of row.
Repeat the last six rows until you have worked 10 patterns or length desired.
Row 61: Work shoulder, (k6, p6) twice, turn, knit back.
Row 63: K6, p6, k6, p4, p2 tog, turn, knit back.
Row 65: P6, k6, p6, k3, k2 tog, turn, knit back.
Continue decreasing 1st at neck in every alternate row, keeping pattern correct, until there are 16 sts on needle. Work 8 rows in pattern on the 16 sts.
Cast off.
Cast off 12 sts across centre, k5, p6, k6, p6. Work to correspond with other shoulder. Cast off.
Work the other side to correspond.

To make up

Sew shoulder and side seams, leaving space for armholes.
Crochet around neck and armholes (1 dc in 1 st of knitting, miss 1 st, 5 tr in next, miss 1 st), repeat.

MERRIC

Cast on 48 sts.
Row 1: **K2, *m1, k8, m1, k1. Repeat from * to last st, k1.
Row 2: K1, purl to last st, k1.
Row 3: *k2tog, m1, k1, m1, k8, m1. Repeat from * to last 3 sts, k2 tog, m1, k1.
Row 4: As row 2.
Row 5: K1, k2 tog, m1, * k1, m1, k8, m1, (k2 tog, m1) twice. Repeat from * to last 13 sts, k1, m1, k8, m1, k2 tog, m1, k2.
Row 6: K1, p4, *(p4 tog) twice, p7. Repeat from * to last 13 sts, (p4 tog) twice, p4, k1**.
Repeat **–** until work measures 19 cm (7½") or length desired.

The three vests, clockwise from top left in this detail are Merric, Oliver and Jasper.

With right side facing shape armhole thus:
Row 1: Cast off 4 sts (k6, inc in next st) to end of row.
Row 2: Cast off 4 sts, purl to end.
Row 3: Knit.
Row 4: K4, purl to last 4 sts, k4.
Repeat rows 3 and 4 until work measures 21.5 cm (8½″).
Next row: With right side facing, knit.
Next row: K4, p4, k28, p4, k4.
Repeat last 2 rows twice.

Shape neck:
Row 1: K12.
Row 2: K4, p4, k4.
Repeat rows 1 and 2 until work measures 27 cm (10½″).

Front

Work buttonhole row, k3, m1, k2 tog, k2, k2 tog, m1, k3.
Cast off.
Join yarn at front right hand side.
Cast off 20 sts.
Work 12 remaining sts to correspond with other side.
Cast off.

Back

Knit back same as front, omitting buttonholes.

To make up

Press the work lightly. Sew on buttons to correspond with
buttonholes. Work picot edge around armholes and neck
edge thus:
Round 1: * Work 1 dc into each st, repeat from * to end.
Round 2: * 4 ch, sl st into 1st ch, 3 dc. Repeat from *
to end.
Fasten off.

HIGH BOOTS

Cast on 39 sts.
Work 9 rows st, st.
Next row: K2, * k2 tog, m1, k1, m1, k2 tog tbl, k1. Repeat
from * to last st, k1.
Next row: K1, purl to last st, k1.
Next row: K1, k2 tog, * m1, k3, m1, sl 1, k2 tog, psso.
Repeat from * to last 6 sts, m1, k3, m1, k2 tog tbl, k1.
Next row: K1, purl to last st, k1.
Work 8 rows st, st, beginning with knit row.
Next row: K1, * k1, m1, k2 tog. Repeat from * to last
2 sts, k2 tog.
Next row: K13, p12, k13.

Work instep thus:
K25, turn, p12, turn.
Work 22 rows st, st on these 12 sts.
Cut yarn.
With right side of work facing, commencing where 13
sts remained and using same needle, join yarn. Knit up
13 sts along side of instep. K12 across instep sts. Knit
up 13 sts along other side of instep. K13 across remaining
sts (64 sts).
Work 9 rows in garter st.
Proceed as follows:
Row 1: K1, k2 tog, k27, (k2 tog) twice, k27, k2 tog, k1.
Row 2: K28, (k2 tog) twice, k28.
Row 3: K1, k2 tog, k24, (k2 tog) twice, k24, k2 tog, k1.
Row 4: K25, (k2 tog) twice, k25.
Row 5: K24, (k2 tog) twice, k24.
Cast off.

To make up

Sew seams. Work 1 row 1 dc (3 ch, sl st into 1st ch).
Picot around the top. Press lightly. Thread ribbon
through holes at ankle.

BATTENBERG

Cast on 46 sts.
Row 1: Knit.
Row 2: K2, inc 1, k20, inc 1, k2, inc 1, k20, inc 1, k2.
Row 3: Knit.
Row 4: K2, inc 1, k22, inc 1, k2, inc 1, k22, inc 1, k2.
Row 5: Knit.
Continue working last 2 rows, increasing each alternate
row 1 st at each end and 2 sts in the middle of the row
until in the 9th row you knit 62 sts.
Knit 6 rows.
Row 16: K28, k2 tog, k2, sl 1, k1, psso, k28.
Row 17: K27, k2 tog, k2, sl 1, k1, psso, k27.
Row 18: K26, k2 tog, k2, sl 1, k1, psso, k26.
Decrease twice in the middle of every row until row 28.
Row 28: K16, k2 tog, k2, sl 1, k1, psso, k16, (36 sts).
Knit 2 rows.
Row 31: K4, (m1, k2 tog, k2) to end of row.
Knit 3 rows.
Row 35: (K2, p2) to end of row.
Repeat row 35 twice.
Row 38: (P2, k2) to end of row.
Repeat row 38 twice.
Repeat the last 6 rows.
Cast off.
Sew the seams. Thread ribbon through holes at ankle.

SHOES

Cast on 33 sts.
Row 1: Knit.
Row 2: Purl.
Change to 3 mm (11) needles.
Row 1: K1, (m1, k2 tog) to end of row.
Row 2: Purl.
Row 3: Knit.
Repeat rows 2 and 3, 3 times, then row 2 once.
Next row: K24. Turn.
Next row: P15. Turn.
Knit 6 rows (15 sts).
Proceed in pattern.
Row 1: K6, m1, sl 1, k2 tog, psso, m1, k6.
Row 2 and alternate rows: Purl.
Row 3: K5, m1, sl 1, k1, psso, k1, k2 tog, m1, k5.
Row 5: K4, m1, sl 1, k1, psso, k3, k2 tog, m1, k4.
Row 7: K2, k2 tog, m1, k3, m1, sl 1, k1, psso, k2, m1, sl 1, k1, psso, k2.
Row 9: K3, k2 tog, m1, k5, m1, sl 1, k1, psso, k3.
Row 11: K4, k2 tog, m1, k3, m1, sl 1, k1, psso, k4.
Row 13: K5, k2 tog, m1, k1, m1, sl 1, k1, psso, k5.
Row 14: Purl.
Cut yarn. Join yarn to sts on right-hand needle and use the same needle to knit up 15 sts along side of instep. Knit across instep sts. Knit up 15 sts along other side of instep. Knit across remaining 9 sts (63 sts).
Knit 2 rows.

Continue thus:
Row 1 and alternate rows: Knit.
Row 2: K25, k2 tog, k9, k2 tog, k to end of row.
Row 4: K25, k2 tog, k7, k2 tog, k to end of row.
Row 6: K25, k2 tog, k5, k2 tog, k to end of row.
Row 8: K25, k2 tog, k3, k2 tog, k to end of row.
Row 10: K25, k2 tog, k1, k2 tog, k to end of row.
Row 12: K25, sl 1, k2 tog, psso, k to end of row.
Row 14: K2, k2 tog, k to last 3 sts, k2 tog, k1.
Row 15: Knit.
Cast off.

Ankle strap

Using 3 mm (11) needles cast on 5 sts.
Row 1: K1, (p1, k1) twice.
Row 2: P1, (k1, p1) twice.
Repeat rows 1 and 2 until strap measures 5 cm (2″) ending with row 2.
Cast off ribwise.
Sew up foot and leg seams. Turn picot edge to form hem. Slip stitch into position. Stitch ankle strap to front of shoe. Sew a small button at side of strap.

17: UNDERWEAR

Two useful and necessary items in a baby's layette, knitted by Eileen Kerney from 1930s patterns. The soaker is outstandingly simple in design, while the tiny cross over vest suits a baby of one or two months. The postcards in the illustration are from the original drawings of Mary Tourtel.

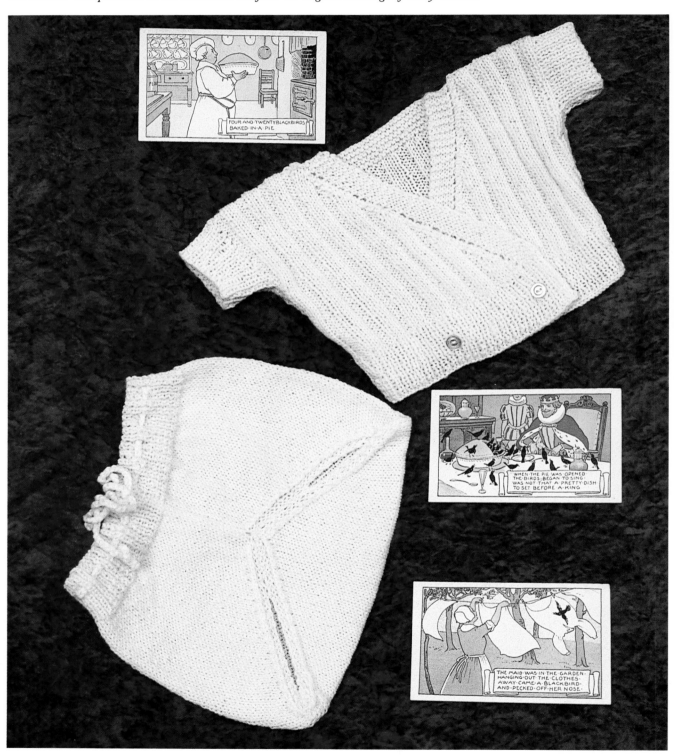

VEST

Materials

1 × 50 g ball 3-ply wool
Needles 3 mm (11)

Back

Cast on 60 sts.
Work 15 rows k1, p1, rib.
With right side facing work pattern rows thus:
Row 1: (K3, p3) to end of row.
Row 2: (P3, k3) to end of row.
Work 18 rows this way, increasing 1 st at beginning of every row and keeping pattern correct (78 sts).
Work 24 rows.
Next row: Work 27 sts in rib pattern, k24, rib 27 sts.
Repeat this row 10 times.
Cast off for back of neck:
Rib pattern 27, cast off 24 sts, rib 27.
Work left side.
At neck border work thus:
Row 1: K5, m1, k2 tog, rib to end of row.
Row 2: Rib to last 7 sts, k twice in next st, k6.
Repeat these 2 rows, 20 times.
Keeping border correct, k2 tog at other end on every row until 50 sts remain.
Work 15 rows, k1, p1, rib.
Cast off.

Work right side to correspond, reversing shaping.

Work band as follows:
Work 7 rows, k1, p1, rib.

Buttonhole band:
Right side facing, rib 6, k2 tog, m1, rib 20, k2 tog, m1, rib to end of row.
Work 7 rows k1, p1, rib.
Cast off.
Sew body, leaving sleeve openings. Pick up sts evenly along sleeve openings and work 12 rows k1, p1, rib.
Cast off. Join sleeve seams. Sew buttons to front band.

SOAKER

(also called pilcher or modesty)

Materials

3-ply baby wool
Needles 2.75 mm (12) and 3.25 mm (10)

Measurements

Waist to crutch 19 cm (7½")
Width at widest part approx. 48 cm (19")

Using 2.75 mm (12) needles, cast on 140 sts.
Work 1.25 cm (½") in k1, p1, rib.
Next row: (K1, p1, m1, p2 tog) to end of row.
Continue in rib until work measures 2.5 cm (1").
Change to 3.25 mm (10) needles work in st, st until work measures 10 cm (4").

Shape thus:
Next row: K2, k2 tog, knit to last 4 sts, k2 tog, k2.
Next row: K2, p2 tog, purl to last 4 sts, p2 tog, k2.
Repeat last 2 rows until 4 sts remain.
Next row: K1, k2 tog, k1, k3 tog. Fasten off.

To make up

Join straight sides to form centre seam. Stitch point to this seam. Sew sloping edges together at each side of centre for about 5 cm (2").
Thread a knitted cord through holes at waist. Tie into bow. Stitching firmly through cord and centre back prevents cord slipping through holes.

18: BARBARA'S BIB

A small bib for special occasions, worked by Barbara Hosking from a nineteenth century chin cloth pattern.

Materials

1 × 20 g ball DMC 20 cotton
Needles 1.25 mm (18)
Narrow ribbon
DMC embroidery thread for rosebuds

Cast on 55 sts.
Knit 5 rows.
Row 6: K3, (m2, k2tog). Repeat to last 2 sts, k2.
Row 7: K4, (drop 2nd loop, k2). Repeat to end of row.
Rows 8 and 9: Knit.
Row 10: K3, m2, k2tog, k to last 4 sts, m2, k2tog, k2.
Row 11: K4, drop 2nd loop of m2 of previous row, k to last 4 sts, drop 2nd loop, k3.
Row 12: Knit. (K2tog) in the centre of row.

Row 13: K7, p to last 7 sts, k7.
Row 14: As row 10.
Row 15: K4, drop 2nd loop, k3, p to last 7 sts, k4, drop 2nd loop, k3.
Rows 16 and 17: Knit.
Row 18: K3, m2, k2tog, k2, p to last 7 sts, k3, m2, k2tog, k2.
Row 19: K4, drop 2nd loop, k to last 4 sts, drop 2nd loop, k3.
Continue working in 5 rows of reversed st, st followed by 5 rows st, st and keeping the 7 border sts each end garter st. Make ribbon holes as before in every 4th row and decrease in centre by k2 tog every 10th row until there are 7 reversed st, st bands and 8 st, st bands.
Next row: K3, m2, k2tog, k2, cast off until last 6 sts, k2, (counting last cast-off st) m2, k2tog, k2.
Row 1: ** K4, drop 2nd loop, k2.
Rows 2 and 3: Knit.
Row 4: K3, m2, k2tog, k2 **.
Repeat from **–** until there are 17 ribbon holes.
Knit 3 rows.
K2tog at each end of next 2 rows.
Cast off.
Work other strap to correspond.

Edging

Cast on 4 sts.
Row 1: K1, p3.
Row 2: K1, m1, k1 tbl, m1, sl 1, k1, psso.
Row 3: K1, p2, (k1, p1, k1, p1) into next st, p1.
Row 4: Cast off 4 sts, k1, m1, sl 1, k1, psso.
Repeat rows 1–4 until length required to go around bib, easing at top of strap and joining on second strap. Thread narrow ribbon through holes, leaving both ends to tie at back of neck. Stitch strap to ribbon to hold in place. Embroider tiny rosebuds.

19: EARLY ARRIVALS

These three tiny jackets are all sized for very tiny babies; in fact, can all be worn by premature babies. From bottom to top, they are Sharlene, Penny and Kate.

SHARLENE

This tiny jacket (at the bottom of the picture), would make a charming gift. It was knitted by Edna Lomas and embroidered by Joan Jackson.
The ribbons are threaded through the lace design and can be removed to allow for the child's growth.

Materials

2 × 50 g balls of 4-ply cotton
Needles 2.75 mm (12)
DMC embroidery thread
Ribbon for waist and sleeves
7 small buttons

Measurements

Length from shoulder approx 23 cm (9″)
Chest 53 cm (21″)
Sleeves 15 cm (6″)
Tension 8½ sts to 2.5 cm (1″)

Back

Cast on 85 sts.
Work in moss st for 8 rows, increasing 1 st at end of last row.
Work in pattern thus:
Row 1: K1, (m1, k2 tog, k2) to last st, k1.
Row 2: P2, (p2 tog, m1, p2) to end of row.
Row 3: K3, (m1, k2 tog, k2) to last 3 sts, m1, k2 tog, k1.
Row 4: (P2 tog, m1, p2) to last 2 sts, p2.
Row 5: K3, (k2 tog, m1, k2) to last 3 sts, k2 tog, m1, k1.
Row 6: (P2, m1, p2 tog) to last 2 sts, p2.
Row 7: K1, (k2 tog, m1, k2) to last st, k1.
Row 8: P4, (m1, p2 tog, p2). Repeat to last 2 sts, m1, p2 tog.
Repeat rows 1–8 until work measures approx. 15 cm (6″) or length desired from beginning, ending with row 8.

Armhole shaping:
Cast off 4 sts at beginning of next 4 rows. Continue on remaining sts until back measures 23 cm (9″).
Cast off.

Right front

Cast on 49 sts.
Work 6 rows moss st.
Row 7: Moss st 4, m1, k2 tog. Moss st to end of row.
Row 8: Moss st.
Next row: Moss st 7, then sl these 7 sts onto a piece of thread.

Continue in pattern as given for back on the remaining 42 sts until work measures 15 cm (6″) or length desired from beginning, ending with right side row.

Armhole shaping:
Cast off 4 sts at beginning of next row and next alternate row. Continue on remaining sts until work measures 19 cm (7½″) from beginning, ending with wrong side row.

Neck shaping:
Cast off 4 sts at beginning of next row and every alternate row until 18 sts remain. Continue on these sts until work measures 23 cm (9″) from beginning.
Cast off.
Slip the 7 sts of front border onto a needle.
Continue in moss st making buttonholes thus: k3, m1, k2 tog, k2, 2.5 cm (1″) apart until you have worked 6 and border is same length to neck as front edge, ending with wrong side row. Leave the 7 sts on spare needle.

Left front

Cast on 49 sts. Work 8 rows moss st.
Next row: Work in pattern to last 7 sts. Turn, leaving the 7 sts on a piece of thread.
Continue in pattern on remaining 42 sts. Work to correspond with right front with all shapings at opposite edges, omitting buttonholes in border.

Sleeves

Cast on 33 sts. Work 7 rows moss st.
Next row: Moss st 4, (k twice in next st) 25 times, moss st 4 (58 sts).
Work in pattern until sleeve measures 15 cm (6″) or length desired. Shape top by casting off 4 sts at beginning of every row until 10 sts remain.
Cast off.

Neckband

Join shoulder seams with right side facing, moss st the 7 sts of right front border and knit 18 sts along neck edge of right front, 27 sts across back of neck, 18 sts along neck edge of left front, then moss st the 7 sts of left border.
Work 3 rows moss st on the sts.
Make a buttonhole on next row as before.
Work 1 row.
Next row: Moss st 12, k2 tog, p2 tog, moss st 5, p2 tog, k2 tog, moss st 27, k2 tog, p2 tog, moss st 5, p2 tog, k2 tog, moss st 12.
Work 1 row on these sts. Cast off loosely.

To make up

Press jacket on wrong side. Sew in sleeves, then sew side and sleeve seams. Sew borders to front edges. Sew on buttons. Embroider rosebuds on moss st borders. Thread ribbons through pattern at waist and sleeves (these can be removed as the child grows).

PENNY

A tiny jacket for an early arrival, knitted by Edna Lomas. It appears in the middle of the picture.

Materials

2 × 20 g balls DMC 20 cotton
Needles 2 mm (14) for the ribbing and 2.25 mm (13) for rest of jacket
Narrow ribbon to thread through at wrist, waist and neck
4 small buttons

Measurements

Underarm 40 cm (15¾")
Neck to hem 16 cm (approx. 6½")
Sleeves 7.5 cm (approx. 3")

Back

Using 2 mm (14) needles cast on 80 sts.
Work 12 rows k1, p1, rib.
Row 13: Knit, inc 1 st (81 sts).
Row 14: Purl.
Proceed in pattern thus, using 2.25 mm (13) needles.
Row 1: K3, (p3, k6) to last 6 sts, p3, k3.
Row 2: P3, (k1, m1, k2 tog, p6) to last 6 sts, k1, m1, k2 tog, p3.
Row 3: As row 1.
Row 4: Purl.
Row 5: K7, (p3, k6) to last 11 sts, p3, k8.
Row 6: P8, (k1, m1, k2 tog, p6) to last 10 sts, k1, m1, k2 tog, p7.
Row 7: As row 5.
Row 8: Purl.
Repeat the last 8 rows twice, continue thus.
Row 1: Cast off 3 sts, k9, (p3, k6) to last 15 sts, p3, k12.
Row 2: Cast off 3 sts, p9, (k1, m1, k2 tog, p6) to last 12 sts, k1, m1, k2 tog, p9.
Row 3: K2 tog, k7, (p3, k6) to last 12 sts, p3, k7, k2 tog.
Row 4: Purl.
Row 5: K2 tog, k1, (p3, k6) to last 7 sts, p3, k2, k2 tog.
Row 6: P3, (k1, m1, k2 tog, p6) to last 5 sts, k1, m1, k2 tog, p2.

Row 7: K2 tog, (p3, k6) to last 6 sts, p3, k1, k2 tog.
Row 8: Purl (69 sts).
Row 9: K6, (p3, k6) to end of row.
Row 10: P6, (k1, m1, k2 tog, p6) to end of row.
Row 11: As row 9.
Row 12: Purl.
Row 13: K1, (p3, k6) to last 5 sts, p3, k2.
Row 14: P2, (k1, m1, k2 tog, p6) to last 4 sts, k1, m1, k2 tog, p1.
Row 15: As row 13.
Row 16: Purl.
Repeat the last 8 rows 3 times.
Cast off.

Right front

Using 2 mm (14) needles cast on 46 sts.
Rows 1–12: Repeat 1st 12 rows for the back and make a buttonhole in the 7th row thus: K1, p1, m1, k2 tog, rib to end of row.
Row 13: Knit.
Row 14: P to last 6 sts, k6.
Proceed in pattern thus using 2.25 mm (13) needles:
Row 1: K13, (p3, k6) to last 6 sts, p3, k3.
Row 2: P3, (k1, m1, k2 tog, p6) to last 16 sts, k1, m1, k2 tog, p7, k6.
Row 3: As row 1.
Row 4: P to last 6 sts, k6.
Row 5: K8, (p3, k6) to last 11 sts, p3, k8.
Row 6: P8, (k1, m1, k2 tog, p6) to last 11 sts, k1, m1, k2 tog, p2, k6.
Row 7: As row 5.
Row 8: As row 4.
Repeat the last 8 rows once, making a buttonhole in the 7th row.
Repeat the 8 rows without a buttonhole.
Row 1: Work in pattern to last 15 sts, p3, k12.
Row 2: Cast off 3 sts, p9, (k1, m1, k2 tog, p6), repeat to end of row.
Continue in pattern, dec 1 st at armhole end in next and alternate rows until 40 sts remain.
Work in pattern for 21 rows.
Row 1: Cast off 6 sts, work in pattern to end of row.
Row 2: Work in pattern, dec 1 st at end of row.
Row 3: Cast off 2 sts, work in pattern to end of row.
Repeat the last 2 rows twice.
Continue in pattern, dec 1 st at neck edge of every row until 20 sts remain.
Cast off.

Left front

Using 2 mm (14) needles, cast on 46 sts.
Work as for right front, omitting buttonhole on the 7th row.

Row 13: Knit.
Row 14: K6, purl to end of row.
Proceed in pattern thus using 2.25 mm (13) needles:
Row 1: K3, (p3, k6) to last 16 sts, p3, k13.
Row 2: K6, p7, (k1, m1, k2 tog, p6) to last 6 sts, k1, m1, k2 tog, p3.
Row 3: As row 1.
Row 4: K6, p to end of row.
Row 5: K8, (p3, k6) to last 11 sts, p3, k8.
Row 6: K6, p2, (k1, m1, k2 tog, p6) to last 11 sts, k1, m1, k2 tog, p8.
Row 7: As row 5.
Row 8: As row 4.
Repeat the last 8 rows twice.
Continue in pattern, casting off 3 sts at beginning of the next row at armhole edge.
Continue to correspond with right front, omitting buttonholes.

Sleeves

Using 2 mm (14) needles, cast on 48 sts.
Work 12 rows k1, p1, rib.
Row 13: K10, (k twice in next st, k1) to last 10 sts, k twice in next st, k9 (63 sts).
Row 14: Purl.
Change to 2.25 mm (13) needles, work in pattern for the back until work measures 15 cm (6″).
Keeping the continuity of the pattern, cast off 3 sts at the beginning of the next 2 rows, then dec 1 st at each end of every row until 43 sts remain.
Cast off.

To make up

Press lightly. Sew up seams. Insert sleeves. Using 2 mm (14) needles pick up and knit 76 sts around the neck.
Row 1: (K1, p1) to end of row.
Row 2: K1, p1, (m1, k2 tog) to the last 2 sts, k2.
Repeat row 1 twice, cast off.
Thread ribbon through holes, sew on buttons.

KATE

Another jacket styled for a premature baby (at the top of the picture), knitted by Edna Lomas.

Materials

2 × 20 g balls DMC 20 cotton
Needles 2 mm (14) for ribbing and 2.25 mm (13) for rest of jacket
Length of ribbon
6 small buttons

Measurements

Underarm 40 cm (15¾″)
Neck to hem 16 cm (approx 6½″)
Sleeves 11.5 cm (4½″)

Back

Using 2 mm (14) needles cast on 78 sts.
Row 1: (K1, p1) to end of row.
Repeat this row 11 times.
Next row: K14, (k twice in next st, k15) to end of row (82 sts).
Row 14: Purl.
Change to 2.25 mm (13) needles and proceed in pattern thus:
Row 1: K1, p1, (m1, sl 1, k2 tog, psso, m1, p2) to the last 5 sts, m1, sl 1, k2 tog, psso, m1, p1, k1.
Row 2: K2, (p3, k2) to end of row.
Row 3: K1, p1, (k3, p2) to the last 5 sts, k3, p1, k1.
Row 4: As row 2.
Repeat the last 4 rows 6 times.
Keeping the continuity of the pattern dec 1 st at each end of the next 3 rows, then in alternate rows 3 times.
Work 1 row.
Work 7 patterns.
Cast off.

Right front

Cast on 42 sts on 2 mm (14) needles.
Repeat rows 1–12 of the back, making a buttonhole in the 7th row thus: K1, p1, m1, k2 tog, rib to the end of row.
Row 13: K6, (k twice in the next st, k9) to the last 6 sts, knit twice in the next st, k5 (46 sts).
Row 14: P to last 4 sts, k4.
Proceed in pattern thus:
Row 1: K4, (p2, m1, sl 1, k2 tog, psso, m1) to the last 2 sts, p1, k1.
Row 2: (K2, p3) to the last 6 sts, k6.

Row 3: K4, (p2, k3) to the last 2 sts, p1, k1.
Row 4: As row 2.
Repeat the last 4 rows 6 times.
Make a buttonhole in the 3rd row of the 4th pattern.
Row 1: Work in pattern to the last 7 sts, p2, m1, sl 1, k2 tog, psso, k2 tog.
Row 2: P2 tog, p1, work in pattern to the end of row.
Row 3: Work in pattern to the last 4 sts, p2, k2 tog.
Row 4: K3, p3, (k2, p3) to the last 6 sts, k6.
Row 5: K4, (p2, m1, sl 1, k2 tog, psso, m1) to the last 3 sts, p1, k2 tog.
Row 6: (K2, p3) to the last 6 sts, k6.
Row 7: K4, (p2, k3) to the last 2 sts, k2 tog.
Row 8: K1, p3, (K2, p3) to the last 6sts, k6.
Row 9: K4, p2 (m1, sl 1, k2 tog, psso, m1, p2) to the last 4 sts, m1, sl 1, k1, psso, k2 tog.
Row 10: K1, p2, (k2, p3) to the last 6 sts, k6.
Row 11: K4, (p2, k3) to end of row.
Row 12: As row 10.
Row 13: K2, m1, k2 tog, (p2, m1, sl 1, k2 tog, psso, m1) to the last 5 sts, p2, m1, sl 1, k1, psso, k1.
Row 14: As row 10.
Row 15: As row 11.
Row 16: As row 10.
Row 17: K4, (p2, m1, sl 1, k2 tog, psso, m1) to the last 5 sts, m1, sl 1, k1, psso, k1.
Row 18: As row 10.
Repeat the last 4 rows twice.
Proceed as follows:
Row 1: Cast off 6 sts, work in pattern to end of row.
Row 2: Work in pattern to the last 2 sts, k2 tog.
Row 3: Cast off 2 sts, work in pattern to end of row.
Repeat the last 2 rows twice.
Continue in pattern and dec 1 st at neck edge in the next 4 rows (20 sts).
Work 1 row.
Cast off.

Left front

Cast on 42 sts and work as right front for the first 12 rows, omitting the buttonhole.
Row 13: K5, (k twice in next st, k9) to the last 6 sts, k6.
Row 14: K4, purl to the end of the row.
Proceed as follows:
Row 1: (P2, m1, sl 1, k2 tog, psso, m1) to the last 6 sts, p2, k4.
Row 2: K6, (p3, k2) to the end of row.
Row 3: (P2, k3) to the last 6 sts, p2, k4.
Row 4: As row 2.
Continue to correspond with right side, omitting buttonholes, reversing armhole and neck shapings.

Sleeves

Using 2 mm (14) needles, cast on 48 sts.
Work 10 rows k1, p1, rib.
Row 11: K11, (k twice in next st, k2) to the last 13 sts, k twice in the next st, k12 (57 sts).
Row 12: Purl.
Change to 2.25 mm (13) needles, work in back pattern until sleeve measures 15 cm (6″) or length required.
Keeping continuity of pattern, cast off 3 sts at the beginning of the next 2 rows, dec 1 st at each end of every row until 37 sts remain.
Cast off.

To make up

Press lightly, sew up seams, insert sleeves with right side of work facing and using 2 mm (14) needles pick up and knit 76 sts along the neck edge.
Row 1: (K1, p1) to end of row.
Row 2: K1, p1, m1, k2 tog, rib to end of row.
Repeat row 1 twice.
Cast off.
Thread ribbon through holes, sew on buttons.

20: DOMINIC

A basic boy's jumper designed for a 55 cm (22") chest, and knitted by Eileen Kerney in classic navy and red. Choose your neckline—round or polo.

Materials

Approx. 5 × 50 g balls 5-ply wool
Needles 3 mm (11) and 3.75 mm (9)
Tension 8½ sts to 2.5 cm (1″) over st, st

Front

Using 3 mm (11) needles, cast on 81 sts.
Row 1: K2, * p1, k1. Repeat from * to last st, k1.
Row 2: K1, * p1, k1. Repeat from * to end of row.
Repeat rows 1 and 2, 7 times.
Change to 3.75 mm (9) needles. Continue in st, st until work measures 21 cm (approx 10½″), ending with a purl row.

Shape raglan thus:
Cast off 3 sts at beginning of next 2 rows **.
Row 3: K2, sl 1, k1, psso, k to last 4 sts, k2 tog, k2.
Work 3 rows st, st.
Repeat last 4 rows once (71 sts).
Cast off 3 sts at each end of next and alternate rows until 53 sts remain.
Work 1 row st, st.
Shape neck:
Row 1: K2, sl 1, k1, psso, k17, turn.
Continue on these 20 sts.
Row 2: Purl.
Row 3: K2, sl 1, k1, psso, k to last 2 sts, sl 1, k1, psso.
Repeat rows 2 and 3 until 8 sts remain.
Cast off 3 sts at armhole edge, only in alternate rows, until 3 sts remain.
Next row: P3.
Next row: K1, sl 1, k1, psso.
Next row: P2, turn, k2 tog. Fasten off.
Slip next 11 sts onto st holder. Join yarn to remaining sts. Knit to last 4 sts, (k2 tog, k2).
Continue on the 20 sts.
Next row: Purl.
Next row: K2 tog, k to last 4 sts, (k2 tog, k2).
Repeat last 2 rows until 8 sts remain.
Cast off 3 sts at armhole edge, only in alternate rows, until 3 sts remain.
Next row: P3.
Next row: K2 tog, k1.
Next row: P2, turn, k2 tog. Fasten off.

Back

Work as for front until **.
Row 3: K2, sl 1, k1, psso, k to last 4 sts, k2 tog, k2.
Work 3 rows st, st.
Repeat last 4 rows once (71 sts).
Cast off 3 sts at each end of next and alternate rows until 27 sts remain. Work 1 row. Leave sts on holder.

Sleeves (make 2)

Cast on 43 sts.
Work 15 rows in rib as for back.
Next row: Rib 6, * inc in next st, rib 3, repeat from * to last 5 sts. Rib to end of row (51).
Change to 3.75 mm (9) needles.
Work 4 rows st, st.
Row 5: K2, inc 1, k to last 2 sts, inc 1, k2.
Continue in stocking st. Inc as before at each end of following 6th row until there are 61 sts, then in following 8th row until there are 67 sts. Continue without shaping until work measures 23 cm (9″) or length desired, ending with a purl row.

Shape raglan

Cast off 3 sts at beginning of next 2 rows.
Row 3: K2, sl 1, k1, psso, k to last 4 sts, k2 tog, k2.
Work 1 row st, st.
Cast off 3 sts at each end of next and alternate rows until 9 sts remain.
Work 1 row. Cast off.

Neckband

Using back st, join raglan seams, leaving left back raglan open and noting that the tops of the sleeves form part of neckline. With right side facing using 3 mm (11) needles, pick up and knit 104 sts around neck.
Row 1: * K1, p1. Repeat from * to end of row.**
Repeat row 1, 20 times.
Cast off ribwise.

For a polo collar continue from ** thus:
Repeat row 1, 14 times.
Change to 3.75 mm (9) needles.
Repeat row 1 until collar measures 9 cm (3½″) from beginning.
Cast off ribwise.

Make up (round neck jumper)

Using warm iron and slightly damp cloth, press lightly. Using back st, join left back raglan seam. Join side and sleeve seams. Fold neckband in half to wrong side of work. Sl st into position. Press seams.

Make up (polo neck jumper)

Using back st join left back raglan and polo collar seam, reversing the seam at needle change on collar. Fold polo collar in half to right side of jumper.

21: BENDIGO

A delicate one-ply shawl knitted by Dulcie Brewer and Ruth Rintoule from a Barbara Hosking design adapted from an old pattern. Such beautifully fine wool knits up into a lightweight shawl 107 cm (42") square.

Materials

Approx. 200 g (7 oz) 1-ply wool
Needles 2.75 mm (12)

Centre section (make 4)

Cast on 1 st.
Row 1: M1, k1.
Row 2: M1, k2.
Row 3: M1, k3.
Row 4: M1, k4.
Row 5: M1, k5.
Row 6: M1, k6.
Row 7: M1, k7.
Row 8: M1, k8.
Row 9: M1, k2, k2 tog, m1, sl 1, k1, psso, k3.
Row 10: M1, k3, p3, k3.
Row 11: M1, k2, k2 tog, m1, k1, m1, sl 1, k1, psso, k3.
Row 12: M1, k3, p5, k3.
Row 13: M1, k2, k2 tog, m1, k3, m1, sl 1, k1, psso, k3.
Row 14: M1, k3, p7, k3.
Row 15: M1, k2, k2 tog, m1, k5, m1, sl 1, k1, psso, k3.
Row 16: M1, k3, p9, k3.
Row 17: M1, k2, k2 tog, m1, k2 tog, m1, sl 1, k2 tog, psso, (m1, sl 1, k1, psso) twice, k3.
Row 18 and alternate rows: M1, k3, p to last 3 sts, k3.
Row 19: M1, k4, m1, k2 tog, m1, k3, m1, sl 1, k1, psso, m1, k5.
Row 21: M1, k2, k2 tog, m1, k1, m1, k2 tog, m1, k5, m1, sl 1, k1, psso, m1, k1, m1, sl 1, k1, psso, k3.
Row 23: M1, k2, k2 tog, m1, k3, (m1, sl 1, k1, psso) twice, k1, k2 tog, m1, k2 tog, m1, k3, m1, sl 1, k1, psso, k3.
Row 25: M1, k2, k2 tog, m1, k5, m1, sl 1, k1, psso, m1, sl 1, k2 tog, psso, m1, k2 tog, m1, k5, m1, sl 1, k1, psso, k3.
Row 27: M1, k2, k2 tog, m1, k1, * m1, sl 1, k1, psso, k1, k2 tog, m1, k1 *. Repeat from *–* twice, m1, sl 1, k1, psso, k3.
Row 29: M1, k4, m1, k3, * m1, sl 1, k2 tog, psso, m1, k3 *. Repeat from *–* twice, m1, k5.
Row 31: M1, k2, k2 tog, m1, k1, * m1, sl 1, k1, psso, k7, k2 tog, m1, k1. Repeat from * to last 5 sts, m1, sl 1, k1, psso, k3.
Row 33: M1, k2, k2 tog, m1, k3, * m1, sl 1, k1, psso, k5, k2 tog, m1, k3. Repeat from * to last 5 sts, m1, sl 1, k1, psso, k3.
Row 35: M1, k2, k2 tog, m1, k5, * m1, sl 1, k1, psso, k3, k2 tog, m1, k5. Repeat from * to last 5 sts, m1, sl 1, k1, psso, k3.
Row 37: M1, k2, k2 tog, m1, k2 tog, m1, sl 1, k2 tog, psso, m1, sl 1, k1, psso, * m1, sl 1, k1, psso, k1, k2 tog, m1, k2 tog, m1, sl 1, k2 tog, psso, m1, sl 1, k1, psso. Repeat from * to last 5 sts, m1, sl 1, k1, psso, k3.
Row 39: M1, k4, m1, k2 tog, m1, k3, m1, sl 1, k1, psso, * m1, sl 1, k2 tog, psso, m1, k2 tog, m1, k3, m1, sl 1, k1, psso. Repeat from * to last 5 sts, m1, k5.
Row 41: M1, k2, k2 tog, m1, k1, * m1, k2 tog, m1, k5, m1, sl 1, k1, psso, m1, k1. Repeat from * to last 5 sts, m1, sl 1, k1, psso, k3.
Row 43: M1, k2, k2 tog, m1, k3, * (m1, sl 1, k1, psso) twice, k1, k2 tog, m1, k2 tog, m1, k3. Repeat from * to last 5 sts, m1, sl 1, k1, psso, k3.
Row 45: M1, k2, k2 tog, m1, k5, * m1, sl 1, k1, psso, m1, sl 1, k2 tog, psso, m1, k2 tog, m1, k5. Repeat from * to last 5 sts, m1, sl 1, k1, psso, k3.
Row 47: M1, k2, k2 tog, m1, k1, * m1, sl 1, k1, psso, k1, k2 tog, m1, k1. Repeat from * to last 5 sts, m1, sl 1, k1, psso, k3.
Row 49: M1, k4, m1, k3, * m1, sl 1, k2 tog, psso, m1, k3. Repeat from * to last 5 sts, m1, k5.
Row 50: As row 18.
Repeat rows 31–50 until 8 patterns are completed.
Adjust size here if necessary.

Commence 'beading', proceeding as follows:
Rows 1 and 2: M1, k to end of row.
Row 3: M1, k3, p to last 3 sts, k3.
Row 4: M1, k to end of row.
Row 5: M1, k3, (m2, sl 1, k2 tog, psso) to last 2 sts, k2.
Row 6: M1, k4, p1, (k2, p1) to last 4 sts, k4.
Row 7: *M1, k3, m2, sl 1, k1, psso, (m2, sl 1, k2 tog, psso). Repeat from * to last 2 sts, k2.
Row 8: M1, k4, p1, (k2, p1) to last 2 sts, k2.
Row 9: M1, k3, p to last 3 sts, k3.
Row 10: M1, k to end of row.
Row 11: M1, k1, k2 tog, k to last 3 sts, k2 tog, k1.
Row 12: M1, k1, k2 tog, p to last 3 sts, k2 tog, k1.
Repeat rows 11 and 12 until 6 sts remain.

Next row: M1, k1, k3 tog, k2.
Next row: M1, k3 tog.
Next row: K2 tog. Fasten off.
This forms the st, st centre of shawl.

Border for right side (make 4)

Work mitred corner thus:
Cast on 1 st.
Work rows 1–18 of centre pattern.
Row 19: M1, k2, k2 tog, m1, k2 tog, m1, k3, m1, sl 1, k1, psso, m1, k5.
Row 20 and alternate rows: M1, k3, p to last 3 sts, k3.
Row 21: M1, k2, k2 tog, m1, k2 tog, m1, k5, m1, sl 1, k1, psso, m1, k1, m1, sl 1, k1, psso, k3.
Row 23: M1, k1, k2 tog, sl 1, k1, psso, (m1, sl 1, k1, psso) twice, k1, k2 tog, m1, k2 tog, m1, k3, m1, sl 1, k1, psso, k3.
Row 25: M1, k1, k2 tog, sl 1, k1, psso, m1, sl 1, k1, psso, m1, sl 1, k2 tog, psso, m1, k2 tog, m1, k5, m1, sl 1, k1, psso, k3.
Row 27: M1, k1, k2 tog, sl 1, k1, psso, * m1, sl 1, k1, psso, k1, k2 tog, m1, k1. Repeat from * once, m1, sl 1, k1, psso, k3.
Row 29: M1, k1, k2 tog, sl 1, k1, psso, * m1, sl 1, k2 tog, psso, m1, k3. Repeat from * once, m1, k5.
Row 31: M1, k1, k2 tog, sl 1, k1, psso, m1, k1, m1, sl 1, k1, psso, k7, k2 tog, m1, k1, m1, sl 1, k1, psso, k3.
Row 33: M1, k2, k2 tog, m1, k3, m1, sl 1, k1, psso, k5, k2 tog, m1, k3, m1, sl 1, k1, psso, k3.
Row 35: M1, k2, k2 tog, m1, k5, m1, sl 1, k1, psso, k3, k2 tog, m1, k5, m1, sl 1, k1, psso, k3.
Row 37: M1, k2, k2 tog, m1, k2 tog, m1, sl 1, k2 tog, psso, (m1, sl 1, k1, psso) twice, k1, k2 tog, m1, k2 tog, m1, sl 1, k2 tog, psso, (m1, sl 1, k1, psso) twice, k3.
Row 39: M1, k2, k2 tog, m1, k2 tog, m1, k3, m1, sl 1, k1, psso, m1, sl 1, k2 tog, psso, m1, k2 tog, m1, k3, m1, sl 1, k1, psso, m1, k5.
Row 41: M1, k2, k2 tog, * m1, k2 tog, m1, k5, m1, sl 1, k1, psso, m1, k1. Repeat from * once, m1, sl 1, k1, psso, k3.
Row 43: M1, k1, k2 tog, sl 1, k1, psso, * (m1, sl 1, k1, psso) twice, k1, k2 tog, m1, k2 tog, m1, k3. Repeat from * once, m1, sl 1, k1, psso, k3.
Row 45: M1, k1, k2 tog, sl 1, k1, psso, * m1, sl 1, k1, psso, m1, sl 1, k2 tog, psso, m1, k2 tog, m1, k5. Repeat from * once, m1, sl 1, k1, psso, k3.
Row 47: M1, k1, k2 tog, sl 1, k1, psso, * m1, sl 1, k1, psso, k1, k2 tog, m1, k1 *. Repeat from *–* 3 times, m1, sl 1, k1, psso, k3.
Row 49: M1, k1, k2 tog, sl 1, k1, psso, * m1, sl 1, k2 tog, psso, m1, k3 *. Repeat from *–* 3 times, m1, k5.
Row 51: M1, k1, k2 tog, sl 1, k1, psso, m1, k1, * m1, sl 1, k1, psso, k7, k2 tog, m1, k1. Repeat from * once,
m1, sl 1, k1, psso, k3.
Row 53: M1, k2, k2 tog, m1, k3, * m1, sl 1, k1, psso, k5, k2 tog, m1, k3. Repeat from * once, m1, sl 1, k1, psso, k3.
Row 55: M1, k2, k2 tog, m1, k5, * m1, sl 1, k1, psso, k3, k2 tog, m1, k5. Repeat from * once, m1, sl 1, k1, psso, k3.
Row 57: M1, k2, k2 tog, m1, k2 tog, m1, sl 1, k2 tog, psso, m1, sl 1, k1, psso, * m1, sl 1, k1, psso, k1, k2 tog, m1, k2 tog, m1, sl 1, k2 tog, psso, m1, sl 1, k1, psso. Repeat from * once, m1, sl 1, k1, psso, k3.
Row 59: M1, k2, k2 tog, m1, k2 tog, m1, k3, m1, sl 1, k1, psso, * m1, sl 1, k2 tog, psso, m1, k2 tog, m1, k3, m1, sl 1, k1, psso. Repeat from * once, m1, k5.
Row 61: M1, k2, k2 tog, * m1, k2 tog, m1, k5, m1, sl 1, k1, psso, m1, k1 *. Repeat from *–* twice, m1, sl 1, k1, psso, k3.
Row 62: As row 20. This completes corner (46 sts).
Row 63: M1, k1, k2 tog, sl 1, k1, psso, * (m1, sl 1, k1, psso) twice, k1, k2 tog, m1, k2 tog, m1, k3. Repeat from * once, (m1, sl 1, k1, psso) twice, k1, k2 tog, m1, k2 tog, m1, k1, sl 1, k1, psso, m1, sl 1, k1, psso, k3.
Row 65: M1, k1, k2 tog, sl 1, k1, psso, * m1, sl 1, k1, psso, m1, sl 1, k2 tog, psso, m1, k2 tog, m1, k5. Repeat from * once, m1, sl 1, k1, psso, m1, sl 1, k2 tog, psso, m1, k2 tog, m1, k2, sl 1, k1, psso, m1, sl 1, k1, psso, k3.
Row 67: M1, k1, k2 tog, sl 1, k1, psso, * m1, sl 1, k1, psso, k1, k2 tog, m1, k1 *. Repeat from *– 4 times, m1, (sl 1, k1, psso) twice, m1, sl 1, k1, psso, k3.
Row 69: M1, k1, k2 tog, sl 1, k1, psso, * m1, sl 1, k2 tog, psso, m1, k3 *. Repeat from *–* 4 times, m1, sl 1, k2 tog, psso, m1, sl 1, k1, psso, k3.
Row 71: M1, k1, k2 tog, sl 1, k1, psso, * m1, k1, m1, sl 1, k1, psso, k7, k2 tog. Repeat from * once, m1, k1, m1, sl 1, k1, psso, k3, sl 1, k1, psso, m1, sl 1, k1, psso, k3.
Row 73: M1, k2, k2 tog, * m1, k3, m1, sl 1, k1, psso, k5, k2 tog. Repeat from * once, m1, k3, m1, sl 1, k1, psso, k2, sl 1, k1, psso, m1, sl 1, k1, psso, k3.
Row 75: M1, k2, k2 tog, * m1, k5, m1, sl 1, k1, psso, k3, k2 tog. Repeat from * once, m1, k5, m1, sl 1, k1, psso, k1, sl 1, k1, psso, m1, sl 1, k1, psso, k3.
Row 77: M1, k2, k2 tog, * m1, k2 tog, m1, sl 1, k2 tog, psso, (m1, sl 1, k1, psso) twice, k1, k2 tog. Repeat from * once, m1, k2 tog, m1, sl 1, k2 tog, psso, (m1, sl 1, k1, psso) twice, sl 1, k1, psso, m1, sl 1, k1, psso, k3.
Row 79: M1, k2, k2 tog, * m1, k2 tog, m1, k3, m1, sl 1, k1, psso, m1, sl 1, k2 tog, psso *. Repeat from *–* twice, m1, sl 1, k1, psso, k3.
Row 81: M1, k2, k2 tog, * m1, k2 tog, m1, k5, m1, sl 1, k1, psso, m1, k1. Repeat from * once, m1, k2 tog, m1, k5, (m1, sl 1, k1, psso) 3 times, k3.
Repeat from row 63 to row 82 until length required, allowing for easement on each side and ending border on row 70. Leave sts on spare needle for grafting (see Techniques, page 11).

Mitred border for left side (make 4)

Cast on 1 st.
Row 1: M1, k1.
Row 2: M1, k2.
Row 3: M1, k3.
Row 4: M1, k4.
Row 5: M1, k5.
Row 6: M1, k6.
Row 7: M1, k7.
Row 8: M1, k2, k2 tog, m1, sl 1, k1, psso, k2.
Row 9: M1, k2, p3, k3.
Row 10: M1, k2, k2 tog, m1, k1, m1, sl 1, k1, psso, k2.
Row 11: M1, k2, p5, k3.
Row 12: M1, k2, k2 tog, m1, k3, m1, sl 1, k1, psso, k2.
Row 13: M1, k2, p7, k3.
Row 14: M1, k2, k2 tog, m1, k5, m1, sl 1, k1, psso, k2.
Row 15: M1, k2, p9, k3.
Row 16: M1, k2, k2 tog, m1, k2 tog, m1, sl 1, k2 tog, psso, (m1, sl 1, k1, psso) twice, k2.
Row 17 and alternate rows: M1, k2, p to last 3 sts, k3.
Row 18: M1, k4, m1, k2 tog, m1, k3, (m1, sl 1, k1, psso) twice, k2.
Row 20: M1, k2, k2 tog, m1, k1, m1, k2 tog, m1, k5, (m1, sl 1, k1, psso) twice, k2.
Row 22: M1, k2, k2 tog, m1, k3, (m1, sl 1, k1, psso) twice, k1, k2 tog, (m1, k2 tog) twice, k2 tog, k1.
Row 24: M1, k2, k2 tog, m1, k5, m1, sl 1, k1, psso, m1, sl 1, k2 tog, psso, (m1, k2 tog) twice, k2 tog, k1.
Row 26: M1, k2, k2 tog, * m1, k1, m1, sl 1, k1, psso, k1, k2 tog. Repeat from * once, m1, (k2 tog) twice, k1.
Row 28: M1, k4, * m1, k3, m1, sl 1, k2 tog, psso. Repeat from * once, m1, (k2 tog) twice, k1.
Row 30: M1, k2, k2 tog, m1, k1, m1, sl 1, k1, psso, k7, k2 tog, m1, k1, m1, (k2 tog) twice, k1.
Row 32: M1, k2, k2 tog, m1, k3, m1, sl 1, k1, psso, k5, k2 tog, m1, k3, m1, sl 1, k1, psso, k2.
Row 34: M1, k2, k2 tog, m1, k5, m1, sl 1, k1, psso, k3, k2 tog, m1, k5, m1, sl 1, k1, psso, k2.
Row 36: M1, k2, k2 tog, m1, k2 tog, m1, sl 1, k2 tog, psso, (m1, sl 1, k1, psso) twice, k1, k2 tog, m1, k2 tog, m1, sl 1, k2 tog, psso, (m1, sl 1, k1, psso) twice, k2.
Row 38: M1, k4, m1, k2 tog, m1, k3, m1, sl 1, k1, psso, m1, sl 1, k2 tog, psso, m1, k2 tog, m1, k3, (m1, sl 1, k1, psso) twice, k2.
Row 40: M1, k2, k2 tog, * m1, k1, m1, k2 tog, m1, k5, m1, sl 1, k1, psso. Repeat from * once, m1, sl 1, k1, psso, k2.
Row 42: M1, k2, k2 tog, * m1, k3, (m1, sl 1, k1, psso) twice, k1, k2 tog, m1, k2 tog. Repeat from * once, m1, (k2 tog) twice, k1.
Row 44: M1, k2, k2 tog, * m1, k5, m1, sl 1, k1, psso, m1, sl 1, k2 tog, psso, m1, k2 tog. Repeat from * once, m1, (k2 tog) twice, k1.
Row 46: M1, k2, k2 tog, * m1, k1, m1, sl 1, k1, psso, k1, k2 tog *. Repeat from *-* 3 times, m1, (k2 tog) twice, k1.
Row 48: M1, k4, * m1, k3, m1, sl 1, k2 tog, psso *. Repeat from *-* 3 times, m1, (k2 tog) twice, k1.
Row 50: M1, k2, k2 tog, m1, k1, * m1, sl 1, k1, psso, k7, k2 tog, m1, k1. Repeat from * once, m1, (k2 tog) twice, k1.
Row 52: M1, k2, k2 tog, m1, k3, * m1, sl 1, k1, psso, k5, k2 tog, m1, k3. Repeat from * once, m1, sl 1, k1, psso, k2.
Row 54: M1, k2, k2 tog, m1, k5, * m1, sl 1, k1, psso, k3, k2 tog, m1, k5. Repeat from * once, m1, sl 1, k1, psso, k2.
Row 56: M1, k2, k2 tog, m1, k2 tog, m1, sl 1, k2 tog, psso, m1, sl 1, k1, psso, * m1, sl 1, k1, psso, k1, k2 tog, m1, k2 tog, m1, sl 1, k2 tog, psso, m1, sl 1, k1, psso. Repeat from * once, m1, sl 1, k1, psso, k2.
Row 58: M1, k4, m1, k2 tog, m1, k3, m1, sl 1, k1, psso, * m1, sl 1, k2 tog, psso, m1, k2 tog, m1, k3, m1, sl 1, k1, psso. Repeat from * once, m1, sl 1, k1, psso, k2.
Row 60: M1, k2, k2 tog, * m1, k1, m1, k2 tog, m1, k5, m1, sl 1, k1, psso *. Repeat from *-* twice, m1, sl 1, k1, psso, k2.
Row 61: As row 17.
Mitre completed.

Continue working straight border thus:
Row 62: M1, k2, k2 tog, m1, k2 tog, k1, (m1, sl 1, k1, psso) twice, k1, k2 tog, m1, k2 tog, * m1, k3, (m1, sl 1, k1, psso) twice, k1, k2 tog, m1, k2 tog. Repeat from * once, m1, (k2 tog) twice, k1.
Row 64: M1, k2, k2 tog, m1, k2 tog, k2, m1, sl 1, k1, psso, m1, sl 1, k2 tog, psso, m1, k2 tog, * m1, k5, m1, sl 1, k1, psso, m1, sl 1, k2 tog, psso, m1, k2 tog. Repeat from * once, m1, (k2 tog) twice, k1.
Row 66: M1, k2, k2 tog, m1, (k2 tog) twice, * m1, k1, m1, sl 1, k1, psso, k1, k2 tog *. Repeat from *-* 4 times, m1, (k2 tog) twice, k1.
Row 68: M1, k2, k2 tog, m1, k3 tog, * m1, k3, m1, sl 1, k2 tog, psso *. Repeat from *-* 4 times, m1, (k2 tog) twice, k1.
Row 70: M1, k2, k2 tog, m1, k2 tog, k3, k2 tog, m1, k1, * m1, sl 1, k1, psso, k7, k2 tog, m1, k1. Repeat from * once, m1, (k2 tog) twice, k1.
Row 72: M1, k2, k2 tog, m1, k2 tog, k2, k2 tog, m1, k3, * m1, sl 1, k1, psso, k5, k2 tog, m1, k3. Repeat from * once, m1, sl 1, k1, psso, k2.
Row 74: M1, k2, k2 tog, m1, k2 tog, k1, k2 tog, m1, k5, * m1, sl 1, k1, psso, k3, k2 tog, m1, k5. Repeat from * once, m1, sl 1, k1, psso, k2.
Row 76: M1, k2, k2 tog, m1, (k2 tog) twice, m1, k2 tog, m1, sl 1, k2 tog, psso, m1, sl 1, k1, psso, * m1, sl 1, k1, psso, k1, k2 tog, m1, k2 tog, m1, sl 1, k2 tog, psso, m1, sl 1, k1, psso. Repeat from * once, m1, sl 1, k1, psso, k2.

Row 78: M1, k2, k2 tog, m1, k3 tog, m1, k2 tog, m1, k3, m1, sl 1, k1, psso, * m1, sl 1, k2 tog, psso, m1, k2 tog, m1, k3, m1, sl 1, k1, psso. Repeat from * once, m1, sl 1, k1, psso, k2.

Row 80: M1, k2, k2 tog, (m1, k2 tog) twice, m1, k5, m1, sl 1, k1, psso, * m1, k1, m1, k2 tog, m1, k5, m1, sl 1, k1, psso. Repeat from * once, m1, sl 1, k1, psso, k2.

Row 81: As row 17.

Repeat rows 62–81 until work measures the same as right side border, ending with row 69. The two borders are grafted together to form a right angle.

To make up

Using the diagram as a guide, join the 4 centre sections and the 4 mitred corners of the shawl, using herringbone st.

The left and right sides of borders are grafted together. Repeat the grafting on the other 3 sides.

Attach the borders to the centre of the shawl by herringbone loops.

Roll the shawl in a slightly damp towel.

Remove, and pin out to shape.

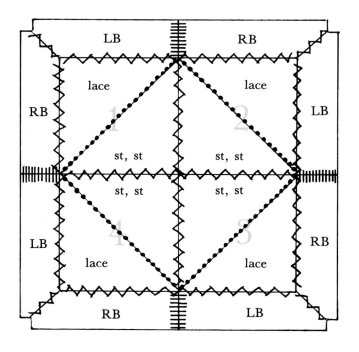

1, 2, 3, 4 = four pieces of centre section

RB = right sides of border

LB = left sides of border

●●●●● = 'beading'

∿∿∿ = herringbone loops/stitch

╫╫╫╫ = grafting

22: BURNOUS

This beautiful lacy cape with frilled hood was designed and knitted by Kathy Grin. Suitable for babies twelve to eighteen months old, it is worn by Annalise O'Toole over the all-in-one Siren Suit (page 52). Patchwork quilt by Joan Jackson.

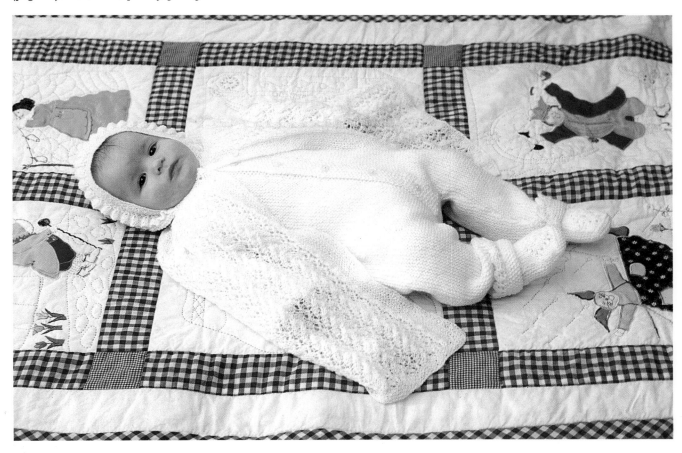

Materials

120 g 2-ply wool
Needles 2 mm (14) and 2.75 mm (12)
3 small buttons

Cape

Cast on 289 sts.
Work 8 rows moss st.
Row 1: Moss st 9, k2, * m1, k2 tog, (m1, k1) twice, k2 tog, k2, k2 tog, k1. Repeat from * to last 14 sts (m1, k2 tog) twice, k1, moss st 9.
Row 2 and alternate rows: Moss st 9, purl to last 9 sts, moss st 9.
Row 3: Moss st 9, k2, * m1, k2 tog, m1, k3, m1, k1, (k2 tog) twice, k1. Repeat from * to last 14 sts, (m1, k2 tog) twice, k1, moss st 9.
Row 5: Moss st 9, k1, k2 tog, * m1, k2 tog, m1, k1, k2 tog, k2, k2 tog, k1, m1, k1. Repeat from * to last 13 sts, m1, k2 tog, m1, k2, moss st 9.
Row 7: Moss st 9, k1, k2 tog, * m1, k2 tog, m1, k1, (k2 tog) twice, k1, m1, k3. Repeat from * to last 13 sts, m1, k2 tog, m1, k2, moss st 9.
Row 8: Moss st 9. Purl to last 9 sts, moss st 9.
Repeat rows 1–8 until work measures 38 cm (15"), ending with row 1.
Next row: (K1, p1) 4 times, p9, * p2 tog, p20. Repeat from * to last 8 sts, (p1, k1) 4 times (277 sts).
Continue thus:
Row 1: (K1, p1) 5 times, * k2 tog, p1, k1, p1. Repeat from * to last 12 sts, k2 tog, (p1, k1) 5 times.
Row 2: * K1, p1. Repeat from * to last st, k1.
Row 3: K1, p1, k2 tog, m2, k2 tog, k1, p1 to end of row.

Row 4: Moss st to end of row, k twice in m2 of previous row.
Work 3 rows moss st.
Row 8: (K1, p1) 5 times, * k2 tog, p2 tog, k1, p1. Repeat from * to last 11 sts, moss st 11.
Work 4 rows moss st.
Row 13: As row 3.
Row 14: As row 4.
Row 15: (K1, p1) 4 times, * k2 tog, p2 tog, k1, p1. Repeat from * to last 11 sts, k2 tog, p2 tog, moss st 7.
Work 7 rows moss st.
Row 23: As row 3.
Row 24: As row 4.
Row 25: Moss st 14, * p2 tog, k1, p1. Repeat from * to last 15 sts, moss st 15.
Cast off.

Hood

Cast on 91 sts.
Row 1: (K1, p1) to last st, k1.
Repeat row 1, 9 times.
Work rows 1–8 of cape pattern 7 times.
Continue thus:.
Rows 1 and 2: Work in pattern to last 10 sts.
Rows 3 and 4: Work in pattern to last 18 sts.
Rows 5 and 6: Work in pattern to last 26 sts.
Rows 7 and 8: Work in pattern to last 34 sts.

Rows 9 and 10: Work in pattern to last 42 sts.
Row 11: Knit.
Row 12: Purl.
Cast off.

Frill

Cast on 7 sts.
Row 1: Knit.
Row 2: K2, p5.
Row 3: K5, turn, p5.
Row 4: K6, turn, k1, p5.
Row 5: P5, k2.
Row 6: Knit.
Row 7: P5, k5.
Row 8: P5, k1, turn, k6.
Repeat rows 1–8 until length required to trim hood.
Cast off.

To make up

Press work under damp cloth with a warm iron. Sew up seam of hood. Stitch hood to cape 2.5 cm (1″) from cape edges. Sew frill along front of hood at the beginning of lace pattern. Sew on buttons to correspond with buttonholes.

23: LULLABY

A small cradle cover from a late nineteenth century design, knitted by Ruth Rintoule.

Materials

6 balls 4-ply cotton
Needles 2 mm (14)
Ribbon for the bows at each corner

Measurements

53 cm (approx. 21″) square

Cast on 2 sts.
Row 1: Knit.
Row 2: M1, k2.
Row 3: (M1, k1) 3 times.
Row 4: M1, k1, p3, k2.
Row 5: M1, k3, m1, k1, m1, k3.
Row 6: M1, k2, p5, k3.
Row 7: M1, k5, m1, k1, m1, k5.
Row 8: M1, k3, p7, k4.
Row 9: M1, k7, m1, k1, m1, k7.

Row 10: M1, k4, p9, k5.

Row 11: M1, k9, m1, k1, m1, k9.

Row 12: M1, k5, p11, k6.

Row 13: M1, k11, m1, k1, m1, k11.

Row 14: M1, k6, p13, k7.

Row 15: M1, k7, sl 1, k1, psso, k9, k2 tog, k7.

Row 16: M1, k7, p11, k8.

Row 17: M1, k8, sl 1, k1, psso, k7, k2 tog, k8.

Row 18: M1, k8, p9, k9.

Row 19: M1, k9, sl 1, k1, psso, k5, k2 tog, k9.

Row 20: M1, k9, p7, k10.

Row 21: M1, k10, sl 1, k1, psso, k3, k2 tog, k10.

Row 22: M1, k10, p5, k11.

Row 23: M1, k11, sl 1, k1, psso, k1, k2 tog, k11.

Row 24: M1, k11, p3, k12.

Row 25: M1, k12, sl 1, k2 tog, psso, k12.

Row 26: M1, k1, p24, k1.

Row 27: M1, k to end of row.

Rows 28 and 29: M1, k1, p to last st, k1.

Row 30: M1, k to end of row.

Row 31: M1, k1, p to last st, k1.

Rows 32 and 33: M1, k to end of row.

Row 34: M1, k1, p to last st, k1.

Row 35: M1, k to end of row.

Row 36: M1, k1, p to last st, k1.

Row 37: M1, k1, (m1, k2 tog). Repeat to last st, k1.

Row 38: M1, k1, p to last st, k1.

Row 39: M1, k1, (m1, k2 tog). Repeat to last st, k1.

Row 40: M1, p to last st, k1.

Row 41: M1, k1, (m1, k2 tog). Repeat to last st, k1.

Row 42: M1, k1, p to last st, k1.

Row 43: M1, k to end of row (44 sts).

Row 44: M1, k1, p to last st, k1.

Row 45: M1, k to end of row.

Rows 46 and 47: M1, k1, p to last st, k1.

Row 48: M1, k to end of row.

Row 49: M1, k1, p to last st, k1.

Rows 50 and 51: M1, k to end of row.

Row 52: M1, k1, p to last st, k1.

Row 53: M1, k to end of row.

Row 54: M1, k1, p to last st, k1 (55 sts).

Row 55: M1, k1, (m1, k1, m1, k9) twice, m1, k1, m1, k10, (m1, k1, m1, k9) twice, m1, k1, m1, k2.

Row 56: M1, k2, (p3, k9) twice, p3, k10, (p3, k9) twice, p3, k2.

Row 57: M1, k3, (m1, k1, m1, k11) twice, m1, k1, m1, k12, (m1, k1, m1, k11) twice, m1, k1, m1, k4.

Row 58: M1, k3, (p5, k9) twice, p5, k10 (p5, k9) twice, p5, k3.

Row 59: M1, k5, (m1, k1, m1, k13) twice, m1, k1, m1, k14, (m1, k1, m1, k13) twice, m1, k1, m1, k6.

Row 60: M1, k4, (p7, k9) twice, p7, k10, (p7, k9) twice, p7, k4.

Row 61: M1, k7, (m1, k1, m1, k15) twice, m1, k1, m1, k16, (m1, k1, m1, k15) twice, m1, k1, m1, k8.

Row 62: M1, k5, (p9, k9) twice, p9, k10, (p9, k9) twice, p9, k5.

Row 63: M1, k9, (m1, k1, m1, k17) twice, m1, k1, m1, k18, (m1, k1, m1, k17) twice, m1, k1, m1, k10.

Row 64: M1, k6, (p11, k9) twice, p11, k10, (p11, k9) twice, p11, k6.

Row 65: M1, k11, (m1, k1, m1, k19) twice, m1, k1, m1, k20, (m1, k1, m1, k19) twice, m1, k1, m1, k12.

Row 66: M1, k7, (p13, k9) twice, p13, k10, (p13, k9) twice, p13, k7.

Row 67: M1, k7, (sl 1, k1, psso, k9, k2 tog, k9) twice, sl 1, k1, psso, k9, k2 tog, k10, (sl 1, k1, psso, k9, k2 tog, k9) twice, sl 1, k1, psso, k9, k2 tog, k8.

Row 68: M1, k8, (p11, k9) twice, p11, k10, (p11, k9) twice, p11, k8.

Row 69: M1, k8, (sl 1, k1, psso, k7, k2 tog, k9) twice, sl 1, k1, psso, k7, k2 tog, k10, (sl 1, k1, psso, k7, k2 tog, k9) 3 times.

Row 70: M1, (k9, p9) 3 times, k10, (p9, k9) 3 times.

Row 71: M1, (k9, sl 1, k1, psso, k5, k2 tog) twice, k9, sl 1, k1, psso, k5, k2 tog, k10, (sl 1, k1, psso, k5, k2 tog, k9) twice, sl 1, k1, psso, k5, k2 tog, k10.

Row 72: M1, k10, (p7, k9) twice, p7, k10, (p7, k9) twice, p7, k10.

Row 73: M1, k10, (sl 1, k1, psso, k3, k2 tog, k9) twice, sl 1, k1, psso, k3, k2 tog, k10, (sl 1, k1, psso, k3, k2 tog, k9) twice, sl 1, k1, psso, k3, k2 tog, k11.

Row 74: M1, k11, (p5, k9) twice, p5, k10, (p5, k9) twice, p5, k11.

Row 75: M1, k11, (sl 1, k1, psso, k1, k2 tog, k9) twice, sl 1, k1, psso, k1, k2 tog, k10, (sl 1, k1, psso, k1, k2 tog, k9) twice, sl 1, k1, psso, k1, k2 tog, k12.

Row 76: M1, k12, (p3, k9) twice, p3, k10, (p3, k9) twice, p3, k12.

Row 77: M1, k12, (sl 1, k2 tog, psso, k9) twice, sl 1, k2 tog, psso, k10, (sl 1, k2 tog, psso, k9) twice, sl 1, k2 tog, psso, k13.

Row 78: M1, k1, p to last st, k1 (79 sts).

Row 79: M1, k to end of row

Rows 80 and 81: M1, k1, p to last st, k1.

Row 82: M1, k to end of row.

Row 83: M1, k1, p to last st, k1.

Rows 84 and 85: K1, k2 tog, k to end of row.

Row 86: K1, p2 tog, p to last st, k1.

Row 87: K1, k2 tog, k to end of row.

Row 88: K1, p2 tog, p to last st, k1.

Row 89: K1, k2 tog, (m1, k2 tog) to last st, k1.

Row 90: K1, p2 tog, p to last st, k1.

Row 91: K1, k2 tog, (m1, k2 tog) to last st, k1.

Row 92: K1, p2 tog, p to last st, k1.

Row 93: K1, k2 tog, (m1, k2 tog) to last st, k1.

Row 94: K1, p2 tog, p to last st, k1.

Row 95: K1, k2 tog, k to end of row.

Row 96: K1, p2 tog, p to last st, k1.

Row 97: K1, k2 tog, k to end of row.

Row 98: K1, p2 tog, p to last st, k1.
Row 99: K1, p2 tog, p to last st, k1.
Row 100: K1, k2 tog, k to end of row.
Row 101: K1, p2 tog, p to last st, k1.
Rows 102 and 103: K1, k2 tog, k to end of row.
Row 104: K1, p2 tog, p to last st, k1.
Row 105: K1, k2 tog, k to end of row.
Row 106: K1, p2 tog, p to last st, k1.
Row 107: K1, k2 tog, (m1, k2 tog) to end of row.
Row 108: K1, p2 tog, p to last st, k1.
Row 109: K1, k2 tog, (m1, k2 tog) to end of row.
Row 110: K1, p2 tog, p to last st, k1.
Row 111: K1, k2 tog, (m1, k2 tog) to end of row.
Row 112: K1, p2 tog, p to last st, k1.
Row 113: K1, k2 tog, k to end of row.
Row 114: K1, p2 tog, p to last st, k1.
Row 115: K1, k2 tog, k to end of row.
Rows 116 and 117: K1, p2 tog, p to last st, k1.
Row 118: K1, k2 tog, k to end of row.
Row 119: K1, p2 tog, p to last st, k1.
Rows 120 and 121: K1, k2 tog, k to end of row.
Row 122: K1, p2 tog, p to last st, k1.
Row 123: K1, k2 tog, k to end of row.
Row 124: K1, p2 tog, p to last st, k1.
Row 125: K1, k2 tog, (m1, k2 tog) to end of row.
Row 126: K1, p2 tog, p to last st, k1.
Row 127: K1, k2 tog, (m1, k2 tog) to end of row.
Row 128: K1, p2 tog, p to last st, k1.
Row 129: K1, k2 tog, (m1, k2 tog) to end of row.
Row 130: K1, p2 tog, p to last st, k1.
Row 131: K1, k2 tog, k to end of row.
Row 132: K1, p2 tog, p to last st, k1.
Row 133: K1, k2 tog, k to end of row.
Rows 134 and 135: K1, p2 tog, p to last st, k1.
Row 136: K1, k2 tog, k to end of row.
Row 137: K1, p2 tog, p to last st, k1.
Rows 138 and 139: K1, k2 tog, k to end of row.
Row 140: K1, p2 tog, p to last st, k1.
Row 141: K1, k2 tog, k to end of row.
Row 142: K1, p2 tog, p to last st, k1.
Row 143: K1, k2 tog, (m1, k2 tog) to end of row.
Row 144: K1, p2 tog, p to last st, k1.
Row 145: K1, k2 tog, (m1, k2 tog) to end of row.
Row 146: K1, p2 tog, p to last st, k1.
Row 147: K1, k2 tog, (m1, k2 tog) to end of row.
Row 148: K1, p2 tog, p to last st, k1.
Row 149: K1, k2 tog, k to end of row.
Row 150: K1, p2 tog, p to last st, k1.
Row 151: K1, k2 tog, k to end of row.
Rows 152 and 153: K1, p2 tog, p to last st, k1.
Row 154: K1, k2 tog, k to end of row.
Row 155: K1, p2 tog, p to last st, k1.
Rows 156 and 157: K1, k2 tog, k to end of row.
Row 158: K1, p2 tog, p to last st, k1.
Row 159: K1, k2 tog, k to end of row.

Row 160: K1, p2 tog, p to last st, k1.
Row 161: K1, k2 tog, k to end of row.
Row 162: K1, p2 tog, p to last st, k1.
Cast off firmly. This completes one section.
Work 3 more sections. Sew sections together, joining centre leaves and sewing over each loop.

Edging

Cast on 32 sts.
Knit one row.
Row 2: K3, m1, p2 tog, k4, k2 tog, m1, k1, m1, k2 tog, k4, m1, p2 tog, k1, p2, k1, (m1, k1) twice, p2, k2, m2, k2.
Row 3: K3, p1, k4, p5, k3, m1, p2 tog, k13, m1, p2 tog, k3.
Row 4: K3, m1, p2 tog, k3, k2 tog, m1, k3, m1, k2 tog, k3, m1, p2 tog, k1, p2, k2, m1, k1, m1, k2, p2, k6.
Row 5: K8, p7, k3, m1, p2 tog, k13, m1, p2 tog, k3.
Row 6: K3, m1, p2 tog, k2, k2 tog, m1, k5, m1, k2 tog, k2, m1, p2 tog, k1, p2, k3, m1, k1, m1, k3, p2, k2, m2, k2 tog, m2, k2.
Row 7: K3, p1, k2, p1, k4, p9, k3, m1, p2 tog, k13, m1, p2 tog, k3.
Row 8: K3, m1, p2 tog, k1, k2 tog, m1, k7, m1, k2 tog, k1, m1, p2 tog, k1, p2, k4, m1, k1, m1, k4, p2, k9.
Row 9: K11, p11, k3, m1, p2 tog, k13, m1, p2 tog, k3.
Row 10: K3, m1, p2 tog, k2 tog, m1, k9, m1, k2 tog, m1, p2 tog, k1, p2, sl 1, k1, psso, k7, k2 tog, p2, k2, (m2, k2 tog) 3 times, k1.
Row 11: K3, p1, (k2, p1) twice, k4, p9, k3, m1, p2 tog, k13, m1, p2 tog, k3.
Row 12: K3, m1, p2 tog, k2, m1, k2 tog, k5, k2 tog, m1, k2, m1, p2 tog, k1, p2, sl 1, k1, psso, k5, k2 tog, p2, k12.
Row 13: K3, k2 tog, k9, p7, k3, m1, p2 tog, k13, m1, p2 tog, k3.
Row 14: K3, m1, p2 tog, k3, m1, k2 tog, k3, k2 tog, m1, k3, m1, p2 tog, k1, p2, sl 1, k1, psso, k3, k2 tog, p2, k2, (m2, k2 tog) 4 times, k1.
Row 15: K3, (p1, k2) 3 times, p1, k4, p5, k3, m1, p2 tog, k13, m1, p2 tog, k3.
Row 16: K3, m1, p2 tog, k4, m1, k2 tog, k1, k2 tog, m1, k4, m1, p2 tog, k1, p2, sl 1, k1, psso, k1, k2 tog, p2, k15.
Row 17: Cast off 10 sts; k6, p3, k3, m1, p2 tog, k13, m1, p2 tog, k3.
Row 18: K3, m1, p2 tog, k5, m1, sl 1, k2 tog, psso, m1, k5, m1, p2 tog, k1, p2, sl 1, k2 tog, psso, p2, k5.
Row 19: K8, inc 1 by picking up a thread and knitting it, k3 (12 sts on right hand needle), m1, p2 tog, k13, m1, p2 tog, k3.
Repeat rows 1–19 until length required to fit around cover, allowing ample fullness at corners. Trim with ribbon or with cord bows.

24: BERCEUSE

This cradle cover and pillow trimmed with Lines and Squares Lace, beautifully complement the early English oak cradle. The exquisite embroidery was designed by Joan Jackson.

Materials

8 × 50g balls Anny Blatt Coton d'Egypte No. 2
Needles for centre of cover and pillow 3 mm (11), for lace edging 2.75 mm (12)
DMC stranded cotton for embroidery, colours Nos 221, 223, 224, 225, 501, 502, 522

Measurements

Cover 74 cm × 66 cm (29″ × 26″)
Pillow 46 cm × 38 cm (18″ × 15″)

PILLOW

Cast on 79 sts.
Rows 1–4: Work in st, st beginning with k row.
Row 5: K4, (m1, k2 tog) to last 3 sts, k3.
Row 6: Purl.
Row 7: K4, m1, k2 tog, k68, m1, k2 tog, k3.
Repeat rows 6 and 7, 19 times, then row 6 once.
Row 47: K4, (m1, k2 tog) twice, k66, m1, k2 tog, k3.
Row 48 and alternate rows: Purl.
Row 49: K4, m1, k2 tog, k2, m1, k2 tog, k64, m1, k2 tog, k3.
Row 51: K4, m1, k2 tog, k4, m1, k2 tog, k62, m1, k2 tog, k3.
Row 53: K4, m1, k2 tog, k6, m1, k2 tog, k60, m1, k2 tog, k3.
Continue this way, moving the diagonal eyelet holes 2 sts to the left on every right side row, still making eyelet holes at the sides as before, until row 69 has been worked.
Row 70: Purl.
Row 71: As row 5.
Work 5 rows st, st.
Cast off.

Pillow back

Cast on 79 sts.
Work in st, st for 76 rows.
Cast off.

COVER

Cast on 119 sts. Work 2 rows st, st.
Continue eyelet pattern thus:.
Row 1: K4, (m1, k2 tog) to last 3 sts, k3.
Row 2: Purl.
Row 3: K4, (m1, k2 tog, k20) to last 5 sts, m1, k2 tog, k3.
Row 4: Purl.
Rows 5–28: These rows form one pattern. Repeat 6 times then rows 1 and 2.
Knit 1 row.
Cast off.

Back

Cast on 119 sts.
Work in st, st until same length as front.
Cast off.

To make up cover and pillow

Press the work. Embroider as desired. (The chart on page 84 shows the sts used in Joan Jackson's design.) Sew front to back with right sides together. Turn. Press thoroughly, avoiding raised embroidery. Stitch openings or sew on press studs.
Knit sufficient Lines and Squares Lace to trim both cover and pillow, allowing fullness at each corner. A pad of filling can be inserted in cover and pillow if desired.

LINES AND SQUARES LACE

Cast on 14 sts.
Row 1: K2, m1, k2 tog, k1, m1, k2 tog, m1, k7.
Row 2 and alternate rows: Knit.
Row 3: K2, m1, k2 tog, k2, m1, k2 tog, m1, k7.
Row 5: K2, m1, k2 tog, k1, (m1, k2 tog) twice, m1, k7.
Row 7: K2, m1, k2 tog, k2, (m1, k2 tog) twice, m1, k7.
Row 9: K2, m1, k2 tog, k1, (m1, k2 tog) 3 times, m1, k7.
Row 11: K2, m1, k2 tog, k2, (m1, k2 tog) 3 times, m1, k7.
Row 12: Cast off 6 sts, k to end of row.
Repeat rows 1–12 until length desired.

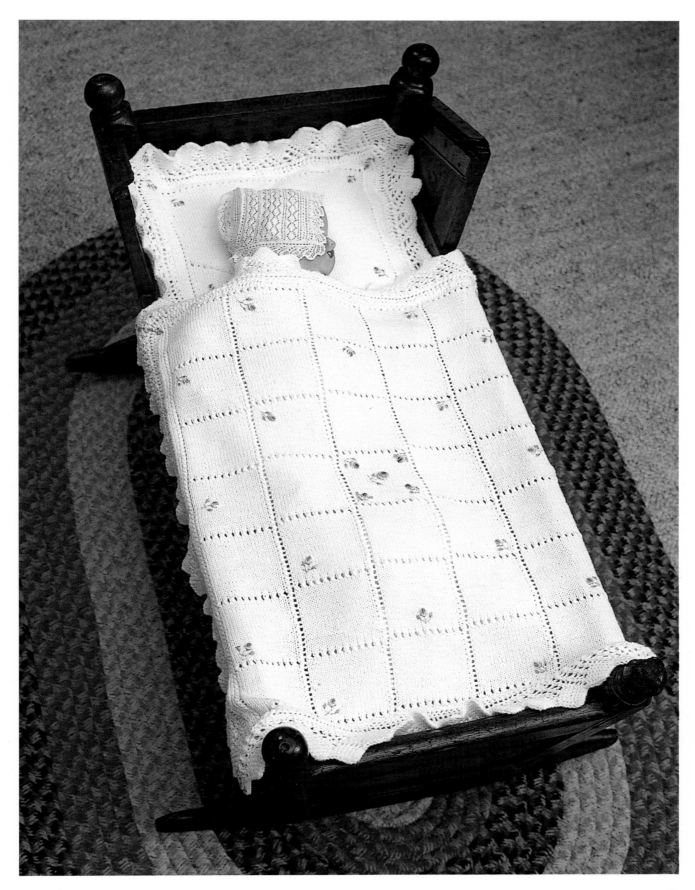

EMBROIDERY STITCHES CHART FOR BERCEUSE

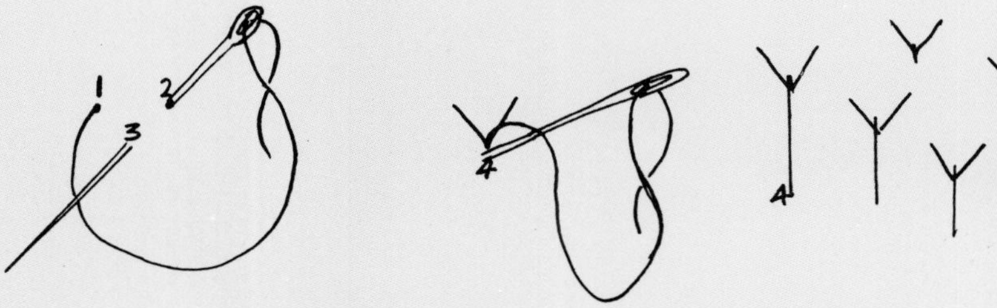

Fly stitch

Elongated fly stitch

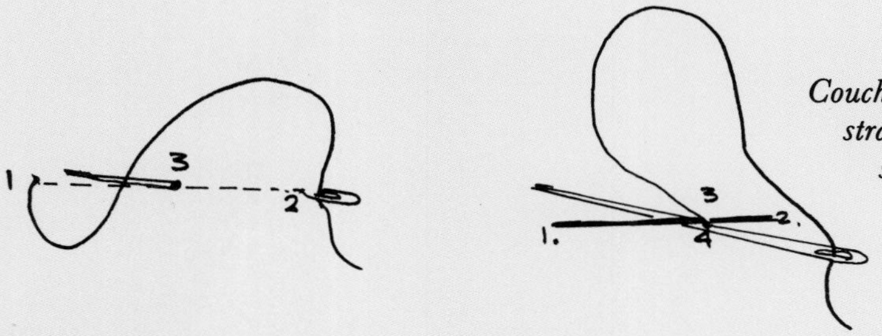

Couched straight stitch

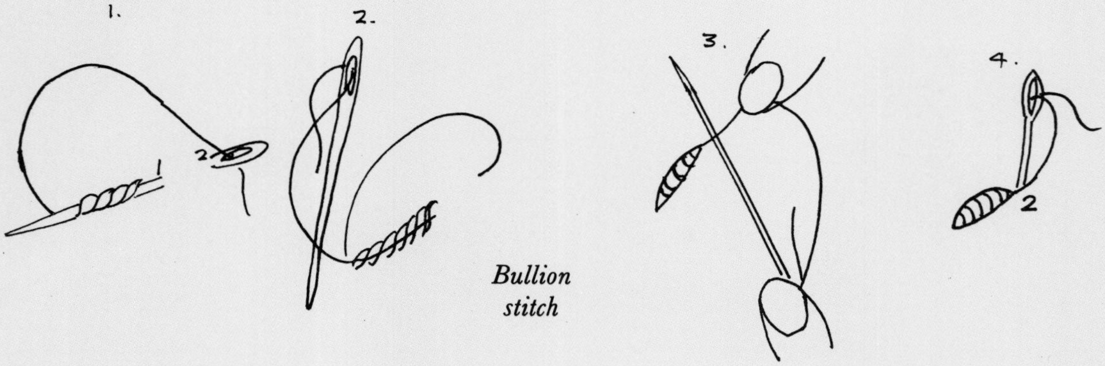

Bullion stitch

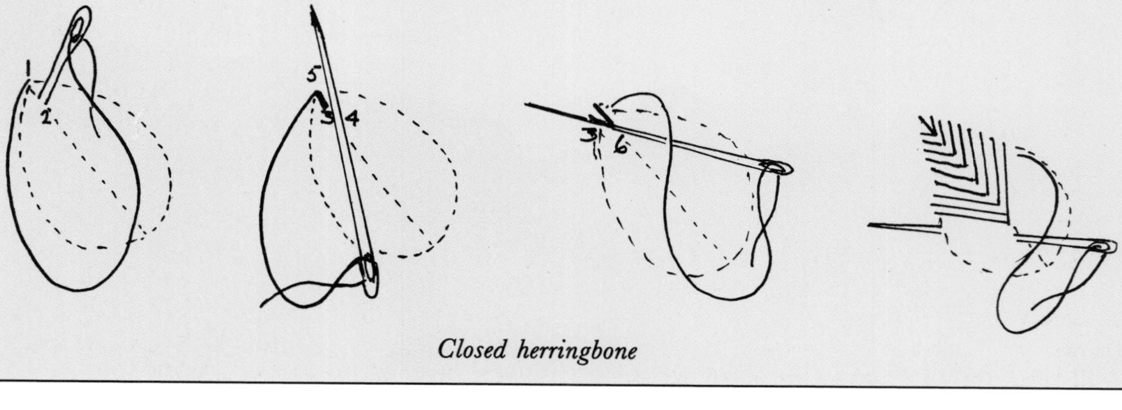

Closed herringbone

25: DULCET

A narrow cover for a cradle or bassinet. The design dates from the late nineteenth century and was knitted by Dulcie Brewer.

Materials

4 × 50 g balls 4-ply cotton
Needles 2 mm (14)

Measurements

70 cm × 44 cm (27½″ × 17¼″)

Cast on 139 sts.
Knit 2 rows.
Row 3: Sl 1, k2, (m1, k2 tog). Repeat until last 2 sts, k2.
Knit 3 rows.
Row 7: As row 3.
Knit 3 rows.
Row 11: Sl 1, k2, (m1, k2 tog) 11 times, k6, k2 tog, m1,
k1, m1, k2 tog, (k7, k2 tog, m1, k1, m1, k2 tog) 6 times, k7, (m1, k2 tog) 11 times, k2.
Row 12: Sl 1, k31, p3, (k9, p3) 6 times, k32.
Row 13: Sl 1, k29, k2 tog, m1, k3, m1, k2 tog, (k5, k2 tog, m1, k3, m1, k2 tog) 6 times, k30.
Row 14: Sl 1, k30, p5, (k7, p5) 6 times, k31.
Row 15: Sl 1, k2, (m1, k2 tog) 11 times, k4, k2 tog, m1, k5, m1, k2 tog, (k3, k2 tog, m1, k5, m1, k2 tog) 6 times, k5, (m1, k2 tog) 11 times, k2.
Row 16: Sl 1, k29, p7, (k5, p7) 6 times, k30.
Row 17: Sl 1, k29, m1, k2 tog, k3, k2 tog, m1, (k5, m1, k2 tog, k3, k2 tog, m1) 6 times, k30.
Row 18: Sl 1, k30, p5, (k7, p5) 6 times, k31.
Row 19: Sl 1, k2, (m1, k2 tog) 11 times, k6, m1, k2 tog, k1, k2 tog, m1, (k7, m1, k2 tog, k1, k2 tog, m1) 6 times, k7, (m1, k2 tog) 11 times, k2.

Row 20: Sl 1, k31, p3, (k9, p3) 6 times, k32.

Row 21: Sl 1, k31, m1, k3 tog, m1, (k9, m1, k3 tog, m1) 6 times, k32.

Row 22: Knit.

Row 23: Sl 1, k2, (m1, k2 tog) 11 times, knit to last 24 sts, (m1, k2 tog) 11 times, k2.

Rows 24, 25, 26: Knit.

Row 27: Sl 1, k2, (m1, k2 tog). Repeat to last 2 sts, k2.

Rows 28, 29, 30: Knit.

Row 31: As row 27.

Rows 32, 33, 34: Knit.

Row 35: Sl 1, k2, (m1, k2 tog) twice, k14, (m1, k2 tog) twice, knit to last 24 sts, (m1, k2 tog) twice, k14, (m1, k2 tog) twice, k2.

Rows 36, 37, 38: Knit.

Row 39: Sl 1, k2, (m1, k2 tog) twice, k14, (m1, k2 tog) twice, knit to last 24 sts, (m1, k2 tog) twice, k14, (m1, k2 tog) twice, k2.

Rows 40, 41, 42: Knit.

Continue thus, working centre pattern of cover:

Row 1: Sl 1, k2, (m1, k2 tog) twice, k4, k2 tog, m1, k1, m1, k2 tog, k5, (m1, k2 tog) twice, k7, k2 tog, m1, k1, m1, k2 tog, (k9, k2 tog, m1, k1, m1, k2 tog) 5 times, k8, (m1, k2 tog) twice, k4, k2 tog, m1, k1, m1, k2 tog, k5, (m1, k2 tog) twice, k2.

Row 2: Sl 1, k11, p3, k18, p3, (k11, p3) 5 times, k18, p3, k12.

Row 3: Sl 1, k9, k2 tog, m1, k3, m1, k2 tog, k14, k2 tog, m1, k3, m1, k2 tog, (k7, k2 tog, m1, k3, m1, k2 tog) 5 times, k14, k2 tog, m1, k3, m1, k2 tog, k10.

Row 4: Sl 1, k10, p5, k16, p5, (k9, p5) 5 times, k16, p5, k11.

Row 5: Sl 1, k2, (m1, k2 tog) twice, k2, k2 tog, m1, k5, m1, k2 tog, k3, (m1, k2 tog) twice, k5, k2 tog, m1, k5, m1, k2 tog, (k5, k2 tog, m1, k5, m1, k2 tog) 5 times, k6, (m1, k2 tog) twice, k2, k2 tog, m1, k5, m1, k2 tog, k3, (m1, k2 tog) twice, k2.

Row 6: Sl 1, k9, p7, k14, p7, (k7, p7) 5 times, k14, p7, k10.

Row 7: Sl 1, k9, m1, k2 tog, k3, k2 tog, m1, k12, k2 tog, m1, k7, m1, k2 tog, (k3, k2 tog, m1, k7, m1, k2 tog) 5 times, k12, m1, k2 tog, k3, k2 tog, m1, k10.

Row 8: Sl 1, k10, p5, k14, p9, (k5, p9) 5 times, k14, p5, k11.

Row 9: Sl 1, k2, (m1, k2 tog) twice, k4, m1, k2 tog, k1, k2 tog, m1, k5, (m1, k2 tog) twice, k5, (m1, k2 tog, k5, k2 tog, m1, k5) 5 times, k2 tog, m1, k6, (m1, k2 tog) twice, k4, m1, k2 tog, k1, k2 tog, m1, k5, (m1, k2 tog) twice, k2.

Row 10: Sl 1, k11, p3, k16, p7, (k7, p7) 5 times, k16, p3, k12.

Row 11: Sl 1, k11, m1, k3 tog, m1, k16, m1, k2 tog, k3, k2 tog, m1, (k7, m1, k2 tog, k3, k2 tog, m1) 5 times, k16, m1, k3 tog, m1, k12.

Row 12: Sl 1, k31, p5, (k9, p5) 5 times, k32.

Row 13: Sl 1, k2, (m1, k2 tog) twice, k14, (m1, k2 tog) twice, k7, m1, k2 tog, k1, k2 tog, m1, (k9, m1, k2 tog, k1, k2 tog, m1) 5 times, k8, (m1, k2 tog) twice, k14, (m1, k2 tog) twice, k2.

Row 14: Sl 1, k32, p3, (k11, p3) 5 times, k33.

Row 15: Sl 1, k32, m1, k3 tog, m1, (k11, m1, k3 tog, m1) 5 times, k33.

Row 16: Knit.

Row 17: Sl 1, k2, (m1, k2 tog) twice, k4, k2 tog, m1, k1, m1, k2 tog, k5, (m1, k2 tog) twice, k14, k2 tog, m1, k1, m1, k2 tog, (k9, k2 tog, m1, k1, m1, k2 tog) 4 times, k15, (m1, k2 tog) twice, k4, k2 tog, m1, k1, m1, k2 tog, k5 (m1, k2 tog) twice, k2.

Row 18: Sl 1, k11, p3, k25, p3, (k11, p3) 4 times, k25, p3, k12.

Row 19: Sl 1, k9, k2 tog, m1, k3, m1, k2 tog, k21, k2 tog, m1, k3, m1, k2 tog, (k7, k2 tog, m1, k3, m1, k2 tog) 4 times, k21, k2 tog, m1, k3, m1, k2 tog, k10.

Row 20: Sl 1, k10, p5, k23, p5, (k9, p5) 4 times, k23, p5, k11.

Row 21: Sl 1, k2, (m1, k2 tog) twice, k2, k2 tog, m1, k5, m1, k2 tog, k3, (m1, k2 tog) twice, k12, k2 tog, m1, k5, m1, k2 tog, (k5, k2 tog, m1, k5, m1, k2 tog) 4 times, k3, (m1, k2 tog) twice, k2, k2 tog, m1, k5, m1, k2 tog, k3, (m1, k2 tog) twice, k2.

Row 22: Sl 1, k9, p7, k21, p7, (k7, p7) 4 times, k21, p7, k10.

Row 23: Sl 1, k9, m1, k2 tog, k3, k2 tog, m1, k19, k2 tog, m1, k7, m1, k2 tog, (k3, k2 tog, m1, k7, m1, k2 tog) 4 times, k19, m1, k2 tog, k3, k2 tog, m1, k10.

Row 24: Sl 1, k10, p5, k21, p9, (k5, p9) 4 times, k21, p5, k11.

Row 25: Sl 1, k2, (m1, k2 tog) twice, k4, m1, k2 tog, k1, k2 tog, m1, k5, (m1, k2 tog) twice, k12, m1, k2 tog, k5, k2 tog, m1, (k5, m1, k2 tog, k5, k2 tog, m1) 4 times, k13, (m1, k2 tog) twice, k4, m1, k2 tog, k1, k2 tog, m1, k5, (m1, k2 tog) twice, k2.

Row 26: Sl 1, k11, p3, k23, p7, (k7, p7) 4 times, k23, p3, k12.

Row 27: Sl 1, k11, m1, k3 tog, m1, k23, m1, k2 tog, k3, k2 tog, m1, (k7, m1, k2 tog, k3, k2 tog, m1) 4 times, k23, m1, k3 tog, m1, k12.

Row 28: Sl 1, k38, p5, (k9, p5) 4 times, k39.

Row 29: Sl 1, k2, (m1, k2 tog) twice, k14, (m1, k2 tog) twice, k14, m1, k2 tog, k1, k2 tog, m1, (k9, m1, k2 tog, k1, k2 tog, m1) 4 times, k15, (m1, k2 tog) twice, k14, (m1, k2 tog) twice, k2.

Row 30: Sl 1, k39, p3, (k11, p3) 4 times, k40.

Row 31: Sl 1, k39, m1, k3 tog, m1, (k11, m1, k3 tog) 4 times, k40.

Row 32: Knit.

Repeat the last 32 rows until you have worked 21 diamonds in the side borders (adjust length of cover here if desired). Repeat the 36 border rows for end of cover. Cast off loosely.

26: SNOWFLAKES

This beautiful cot cover was made by Ruth Tyrie. The snowflake motif is easy and effective.
The lace edging for the cover, also by Ruth, is knitted from the Jessica collar pattern on page 31.
A lace-trimmed sheet and pillowcase set off the cover.

Materials

4-ply cotton (quantity depends on size of cot blanket)
Needles 2 mm (14) for cot cover; 2.75 mm (12) for
    blanket edging
Knitter's needle
Cot blanket

Cast on 1 st.
Row 1: K1, p1, k1 in the st.
Row 2: M1, k3.
Row 3: M1, k4.
Continue thus until there are 24 sts on needle.
Row 23: M1, p24.
Row 24: M1, * k2, m1, k2 tog. Repeat from * 5 times, k1.
Row 25: M1, p26.
Row 26: M1, k27.

Row 27: M1, p28.
Row 28: M1, * k2, m1, k2 tog. Repeat from * 6 times, k1.
Row 29: M1, p30.
Row 30: M1, k31.
Row 31: M1, p32.
Row 32: M1, * k2, m1, k2 tog. Repeat from * 7 times, k1.
Row 33: M1, p34.
Row 34: M1, k35.
Row 35: M1, k36.
Row 36: M1, k37.
Row 37: M1, k38.
Row 38: M1, k39.
Row 39: M1, k40.
Row 40: M1, k41.
Row 41: M1, k42.
Rows 42 and 43: Knit.

Row 44: K2 tog, k41.
Row 45: K2 tog, k40.
Row 46: K2 tog, k39.
Row 47: K2 tog, k38.
Row 48: K2 tog, k37.
Row 49: K2 tog, k36.
Row 50: K2 tog, k35.
Row 51: P2 tog, p34.
Row 52: K2 tog, * k2, m1, k2 tog. Repeat from * 7 times, k1.
Row 53: P2 tog, p32.
Row 54: K2 tog, k31.
Row 55: P2 tog, p30.
Row 56: K2 tog, * k2, m1, k2 tog. Repeat from * 6 times, k1.
Row 57: P2 tog, p28.
Row 58: K2 tog, k27.
Row 59: P2 tog, p26.
Row 60: K2 tog, * k2, m1, k2 tog. Repeat from * 5 times, k1.
Row 61: P2 tog, p24.
Row 62: K2 tog, k23.
Repeat row 62 until 3 sts remain. K3 tog and fasten off.
Repeat from row 1 three times and stitch the 4 pieces together to form a motif.

To make up

The cover is made up of 28 motifs (arranged 7 × 4) and is bordered by a fluted edging 9 cm (3½″) wide, knitted from the Jessica collar pattern on page 31. After assembling the snowflake motifs, sew the fluted edging around the cover, allowing extra fullness at each corner.

Beautiful Snowflakes cot cover complements the nineteenth century cot.

27: BLUEBELL AND FOUNTAIN

Cotton baby blankets edged with Fountain Lace (upper) and Bluebell Lace (lower) make lovely gifts.

Materials

2 cotton blankets
2 balls 4-ply cotton
Needles 2.75 mm (12)
DMC embroidery thread for Bluebell
Sewing cotton and needle

BLUEBELL LACE

Cast on 29 sts.
Row 1: Sl 1, k1, m1, p2 tog, k7, m1, k7, m1, p2 tog, k1, (m2, k2 tog) 3 times, k2.
Row 2: K4, p1, (k2, p1) twice, k1, m1, p2 tog, k15, m1, p2 tog, k2.
Row 3: Sl 1, k1, m1, p2 tog, k5, k2 tog, m1, k1, m1, sl 1, k1, psso, k5, m1, p2 tog, k12.
Row 4: K12, m1, p2 tog, k15, m1, p2 tog, k2.
Row 5: Sl 1, k1, m1, p2 tog, k4, k2 tog, m1, k3, m1, sl 1, k1, psso, k4, m1, p2 tog, k12.
Row 6: K12, m1, p2 tog, k15, m1, p2 tog, k2.
Row 7: Sl 1, k1, m1, p2 tog, k3, k2 tog, m1, k5, m1, sl 1, k1, psso, k3, m1, p2 tog, k12.
Row 8: Cast off 3 sts, k8, m1, p2 tog, k15, m1, p2 tog, k2.
Row 9: Sl 1, k1, m1, p2 tog, k2, k2 tog, m1, k7, m1, sl 1, k1, psso, k2, m1, p2 tog, k1, (m2, k2 tog) 3 times, k2.
Row 10: K4, p1, (k2, p1) twice, k1, m1, p2 tog, k15, m1, p2 tog, k2.
Row 11: Sl 1, k1, m1, p2 tog, k1, k2 tog, m1, k9, m1, sl 1, k1, psso, k1, m1, p2 tog, k12.
Row 12: K12, m1, p2 tog, k15, m1, p2 tog, k2.
Row 13: Sl 1, k1, m1, p2 tog, k2 tog, m1, k11, m1, sl 1, k1, psso, m1, p2 tog, k12.
Row 14: K12, m1, p2 tog, k15, m1, p2 tog, k2.
Row 15: Sl 1, k1, m1, p2 tog, k2, m1, sl 1, k1, psso, k7, k2 tog, m1, k2, m1, p2 tog, k12.
Row 16: Cast off 3 sts, k8, m1, p2 tog, k15, m1, p2 tog, k2.
Row 17: Sl 1, k1, m1, p2 tog, k3, m1, sl 1, k1, psso, k5, k2 tog, m1, k3, m1, p2 tog, k1, (m2, k2 tog) 3 times, k2.
Row 18: K4, p1, (k2, p1) twice, k1, m1, p2 tog, k15, m1, p2 tog, k2.
Row 19: Sl 1, k1, m1, p2 tog, k4, m1, sl 1, k1, psso, k3, k2 tog, m1, k4, m1, p2 tog, k12.
Row 20: K12, m1, p2 tog, k15, m1, p2 tog, k2.
Row 21: Sl 1, k1, m1, p2 tog, k5, m1, sl 1, k1, psso, k1, k2 tog, m1, k5, m1, p2 tog, k12.

Row 22: K12, m1, p2 tog, k15, m1, p2 tog, k2.
Row 23: Sl 1, k1, m1, p2 tog, k6, m1, sl 1, k2 tog, psso, m1, k6, m1, p2 tog, k12.
Row 24: Cast off 3 sts, k8, m1, p2 tog, k7, k2 tog, k6, m1, p2 tog, k2.
Repeat rows 1–24 until desired length.
Stitch to edge of blanket with sewing cotton.

FOUNTAIN LACE

Cast on 25 sts. Knit 1 row.
Row 1: Sl 1, k4, m1, k2 tog, k18.
Row 2: K4, m1, k2 tog, k1, (m1, k2 tog, k2) twice, m2, k2 tog, k3, m1, k2 tog, k3.
Row 3: Sl 1, k4, m1, k2 tog, k3, p1, k4, m1, k2 tog, k5, m1, k2 tog, k2.
Row 4: K4, m1, k2 tog, k5, m1, k2 tog, k8, m1, k2 tog, k3.
Row 5: Sl 1, k4, m1, k2 tog, k8, m1, k2 tog, k5, m1, k2 tog, k2.
Row 6: K4, m1, k2 tog, k1, (m1, k2 tog, k2) twice, (m2, k2 tog) twice, k2, m1, k2 tog, k3.
Row 7: Sl 1, k4, m1, k2 tog, (k2, p1) twice, k4, m1, k2 tog, k5, m1, k2 tog, k2.
Row 8: K4, m1, k2 tog, k5, m1, k2 tog, k10, m1, k2 tog, k3.
Row 9: Sl 1, k4, m1, k2 tog, k10, m1, k2 tog, k5, m1, k2 tog, k2.
Row 10: K4, m1, k2 tog, k1, (m1, k2 tog, k2) twice, (m2, k2 tog) 3 times, k2, m1, k2 tog, k3.
Row 11: Sl 1, k4, m1, k2 tog, (k2, p1) 3 times, k4, m1, k2 tog, k5, m1, k2 tog, k2.
Row 12: K4, m1, k2 tog, k5, m1, k2 tog, k13, m1, k2 tog, k3.
Row 13: Sl 1, k4, m1, k2 tog, k13, m1, k2 tog, k5, m1, k2 tog, k2.
Row 14: K4, m1, k2 tog, k1, (m1, k2 tog, k2) twice, (m2, k2 tog) 4 times, k3, m1, k2 tog, k3.
Row 15: Sl 1, k4, m1, k2 tog, k3, (p1, k2) 3 times, p1, k4, m1, k2 tog, k5, m1, k2 tog, k2.
Row 16: K4, m1, k2 tog, k5, m1, k2 tog, k17, m1, k2 tog, k3.
Row 17: Sl 1, k4, m1, k2 tog, k28.
Row 18: Cast off 10 sts, k19, m1, k2 tog, k3.
Repeat rows 1–18 until length desired.
Stitch to edge of blanket with sewing cotton.

28: CUDDLES

A nineteenth century design for a hot-water bottle cover. The knitting has an interesting texture resulting in a thick soft covering. Cuddles was knitted by Betty Featherstone.
A pair of Point Lace-edged hand towels and four little My Bears (page 105) complete this scene.

Materials for hot-water bottle cover

Approx. 200 g 8-ply cotton
Needles 3.25 mm (10)
4 white buttons

Materials for towel edges

2 balls 4-ply cotton
Needles 2 mm (14)
2 small hand towels

CUDDLES

Cast on 75 sts and work each row thus:
Sl 1, k1, (sl 1 purlwise, m1, k2 tog) to last st, k1.
NB: The sl st must be the m1 of previous row.
Continue until work is long enough to cover both sides of the bottle. Do not cast off.
Proceed as follows:
Fold cover in half. Pick up 75 sts at one side, inserting needle through both edges as you pick up. (This action locks the two sides together.). The 75 sts left on the needle form the border at *one* side of the top opening.
Continue on the 150 sts thus:
Row 1: *Purl.
Row 2: (K4, p2) to end of row.
Row 3: (K2, p4) to end of row.
Row 4: (K2, m1, k2, p2) to end of row.
Row 5: (K2, p5) to end of row.
Row 6: (K2, m1, k1, m1, k2, p2) to end of row.
Row 7: (K2, p7) to end of row.
Row 8: [K2, (m1, k1) 3 times, m1, k2, p2] to end of row.
Row 9: (K2, p11) to end of row.*
Cast off loosely. This completes the border across one edge of top and down one side.
Work the other side thus:
Pick up 75 sts at side, inserting needle through both edges as before. Then pick up 75 sts across the top opening (these are the original cast-on sts) (150 sts).
Work as for other side from *-*.
Cast off loosely.

Straps

Cast on 6 sts.
Commencing with knit row work 26 rows st, st.
Row 27: K3, m2, k2 tog, k1.
Row 28: P3, k1, p3.
Row 29: K2 tog, k3, k2 tog.
Row 30: P2 tog, k1, p2 tog.
Cast off.
Attach straps to cover at each side. Sew buttons to attached ends, and to correspond with buttonholes. Size of cover can be adjusted by number of sts used.

POINT LACE

Cast on 23 sts.
Row 1: Knit.
Row 2: Sl 1, k2, (m1, k2 tog) twice, k3, m1, k2 tog, k2, (m1, k2 tog) 3 times, m1, k2. K in f&b of last st.
Row 3: K25.
Row 4: Sl 1, k2, m1, k2 tog, k1, m1, k2 tog, k2, m1, k2 tog, k3, (m1, k2 tog) 3 times, m1, k3. Knit in f&b of last st.
Row 5: K27.
Row 6: Sl 1, k2, m1, k2 tog, k2, m1, k2 tog, k1, m1, k2 tog, k4, (m1, k2 tog) 3 times, m1, k4. Knit in f&b of last st.
Row 7: K29.
Row 8: Sl 1, k2, m1, k2 tog, k3, (m1, k2 tog) twice, k5, (m1, k2 tog) 3 times, m1, k5. Knit in f&b of last st.
Row 9: K31.
Row 10: Sl 1, k2, m1, (k2 tog) twice, m2, sl 1, k1, psso, k1, m1,.
k2 tog, k6, (m1, k2 tog) 3 times, m1, k6. Knit in f&b of last st.
Row 11: K26, p1, k6.
Row 12: Sl 1, k2, m1, k2 tog, k5, m1, k2 tog, k7, (m1, k2 tog) 3 times, m1, k8.
Row 13: Cast off 11 sts, k22.
Repeat rows 2–13 until length required.
Cast off.
Press lightly. Stitch to towel edge.

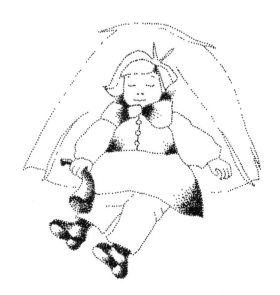

29: CANDY

Knitted towels and face washers make practical presents for a new baby. Patterns date from the nineteenth century knitted by Ruth Tyrie. (Patterns not supplied for discarded clothing.)

Materials

Approx. 4 balls 4-ply cotton make 1 towel and 1 washer
(3 balls white, 1 ball contrast)
Needles 2.75 mm (12)

TOWEL

Cast on 115 sts in white.
Knit 32 rows in white.
Knit 8 rows in pink (or chosen contrast colour).
Knit 8 rows in white.
Knit 8 rows in pink.
Knit 8 rows in white.
Knit 8 rows in pink.
Knit 128 rows in white.
Knit 8 rows in pink.
Knit 8 rows in white.
Knit 8 rows in pink.
Knit 8 rows in white.
Knit 8 rows in pink.
Knit 32 rows in white.
Cast off.

FACE WASHER

Cast on 52 sts.
Knit 8 rows.
Next row: (K1, m1, k2 tog) to last st, k1.
Knit 7 rows.
Next row: (K1, m1, k2 tog) to last st, k1.
Knit 54 rows (adjust size here).
Next row: (K1, m1, k2 tog) to last st, k1.
Knit 7 rows.
Next row: (K1, m1, k2 tog) to last st, k1.
Knit 8 rows.
Cast off.

30: PILLOW PAL

Pillow Pal Bear, simple and effective, is suitable as a gift for a young baby. He stands alongside Bear Track and Winsloe, two baby towels lace trimmed by Joan Eckersley. Pillow Pal was knitted by the author.

Materials for bear

1 × 50 g ball 4-ply cotton
Needles 3.75 mm (9)
Wide ribbon for neck
Fibrefill for stuffing
DMC stranded cotton to embroider face

Measurement

21.5 cm (8½″) high

PILLOW PAL

Ears (make 2)

Cast on 10 sts.
Knit 6 rows.
Row 7: Sl 1, k1, psso, k6, k2 tog.
Row 8: Knit.
Row 9: Sl 1, k1, psso, k4, k2 tog.
Row 10: Knit.
Cast off.

Head and body (in one piece)

Cast on 38 sts.
Knit 30 rows.
Next row: Inc 1 st each end of every alternate row 5 times (48 sts). Divide work and continue knitting each side separately. Work 16 rows.
Cast off.
Work other side to correspond.

Arms (make 2)

Cast on 16 sts.
Knit 10 rows.
Row 11: (K2 tog) to end of row.
Row 12: Knit.
Row 13: (K2 tog) to end of row.
Thread yarn through remaining 4 sts. Draw up and fasten off securely.

Soles (make 2)

Cast on 10 sts.
Knit 12 rows.
Cast off.

To make up

Sew head and body seams. Stuff head and body firmly with filling. Join leg seams. Stuff legs and paws. Sew soles to bottom of legs. Sew arm seams. Stuff firmly and sew to body. Embroider bear's head. Attach ears, curving the tops. Tie wide ribbon around neck and make a bow.

Materials for towels

1 × 50 g ball DMC 10 cotton
Needles 1.75 mm (12)
Hand towels

BEAR TRACKS

Cast on 25 sts.
Knit one row.
Row 1: Sl 1, m1, p2 tog, k1, sl 1, k1, psso, k9, k2 tog, k2, m1, p2 tog, k3, k in f&b of last st (24 sts).
Row 2: K5, m1, p2 tog, p2, p2 tog, k7, sl 1, k1, psso, p1, m1, p2 tog, k1 (24 sts).
Row 3: Sl 1, m1, p2 tog, k1, sl 1, k1, psso, k2, m3, k3, k2 tog, k2, m1, p2 tog, k1, (m2, k2 tog) twice (25 sts).
Row 4: (K2, p1) twice, k1, m1, (p2 tog, p2) twice in the m3 of previous row, (k1, m1) twice, k1, (5 sts out of m3), p1, sl 1, k1, psso, p1, m1, p2 tog, k1 (25 sts).
Row 5: Sl 1, m1, p2 tog, k1, sl 1, k1, psso, k6, k2 tog, k2, m1, p2 tog, k7 (23 sts).
Row 6: Cast off 3 sts, k3, m1, p2 tog, p2, p2 tog, p7, m1, p2 tog, k1 (19 sts).
Row 7: Sl 1, m1, p2 tog, k2, (m1, k1) 6 times, k2, m1, p2 tog, k3, k in f&b of last st (26 sts).
Row 8: K5, m1, p2 tog, p16, m1, p2 tog, k1 (26 sts).
Row 9: Sl 1, m1, p2 tog, k16, m1, p2 tog, k1, (m2, k2 tog) twice (28 sts).
Row 10: (K2, p1) twice, k1, m1, p2 tog, p16, m1, p2 tog, k1 (28 sts).
Row 11: Sl 1, m1, p2 tog, k16, m1, p2 tog, k7 (28 sts).
Row 12: Cast off 3 sts, k3, m1, p2 tog, p16, m1, p2 tog, k1 (25 sts).
Repeat rows 1–12 until lace is length desired.

WINSLOE

Cast on 37 sts.
Knit one row.
Row 1: K2, (m1, k2 tog) twice, m1, k4, k3 tog, k4, (m1, k2 tog) 3 times, m1, k1, m1, k4, k3 tog, k4, (m1, k1) twice (38 sts).
Row 2 and alternate rows: Sl 1, purlwise, p to last 2 sts, k2.
Row 3: K3, (m1, k2 tog) twice, m1, k3, k3 tog, k3, (m1,

k2 tog) 3 times, (m1, k3) twice, k3 tog, (k3, m1) twice, k1 (39 sts).

Row 5: K4, (m1, k2 tog) twice, m1, k2, k3 tog, k2, (m1, k2 tog) 3 times, m1, k5, m1, k2, k3 tog, k2, m1, k5, m1, k1 (40 sts).

Row 7: K5, (m1, k2 tog) twice, m1, k1, k3 tog, k1, (m1, k2 tog) 3 times, m1, k7, m1, k1, k3 tog, k1, m1, k7, m1, k1 (41 sts).

Row 9: K6, (m1, k2 tog) twice, m1, k3 tog, (m1, k2 tog) 3 times, m1, k9, m1, k3 tog, m1, k9, m1, k1 (42 sts).

Row 11: K5, (k2 tog, m1) 3 times, k1, (m1, k2 tog) 3 times, m1, k4, k3 tog, k4, m1, k1, m1, k4, k3 tog, k5 (41 sts).

Row 13: K4, (k2 tog, m1) 3 times, k3, (m1, k2 tog) 3 times, m1, k3, k3 tog, (k3, m1) twice, k3, k3 tog, k4 (40 sts).

Row 15: K3, (k2 tog, m1) 3 times, k5, (m1, k2 tog) 3 times, m1, k2, k3 tog, k2, m1, k5, m1, k2, k3 tog, k3 (39 sts).

Row 17: K2, (k2 tog, m1) 3 times, k7, (m1, k2 tog) 3 times, m1, k1, k3 tog, k1, m1, k7, m1, k1, k3 tog, k2 (38 sts).

Row 19: K1, (k2 tog, m1) 3 times, k9, (m1, k2 tog) 3 times, m1, k3 tog, m1, k9, m1, k3 tog, k1 (37 sts).

Row 20: As row 2.

Repeat rows 1–20 until lace is length desired.

31: COATHANGERS

Three exquisite coathangers designed and knitted by Joan Eckersley make a perfect gift for a baby.
In the centre is Macalie, with a matching towel. At lower left is Crystal, designed to complement a christening gown. Joan, a full size coathanger at the back, is designed as a gift for the new mother.
The bears enjoying the first wattle of the winter are the creations of Kathie Savage (see suppliers, page 119).

Materials

2 × 50 g balls DMC 10 cotton
Needles 2 mm (14)
Ribbon for trimming hooks and threading through hangers

CRYSTAL

Cast on 35 sts.
Knit one row.
Row 1: Sl 1, k5 (m1, k2 tog) 4 times, k5, k2 tog, (m1, k2 tog) 5 times, k4.
Row 2: K34.
Row 3: Sl 1, k2, m1, k2 tog, k9, k2 tog, m2, k2 tog, k5, (m1, k2 tog) 3 times, m1, k2, m2, k2 tog, k in f&b of last st (37 sts).
Row 4: K4, p1, k16, p1, k15.
Row 5: Sl 1, k23, (m1, k2 tog) 3 times, m1, k7 (38 sts).
Row 6: Cast off 2 sts, k35 (36 sts).
Row 7: Sl 1, k2, m1, k2 tog, k9, k2 tog, m2, k2 tog, k7, (m1, k2 tog) 3 times, m1, k2, m2, k2 tog, k in f&b of last st (39 sts).
Row 8: K4, p1, k18, p1, k15.
Row 9: Sl 1, k25, (m1, k2 tog) 3 times, m1, k7 (40 sts).
Row 10: Cast off 2 sts, k37 (38 sts).
Row 11: Sl 1, k2, m1, k2 tog, k9, k2 tog, m2, k2 tog, k9, (m1, k2 tog) 3 times, m1, k2, m2, k2 tog, k in f&b of last st (41 sts).
Row 12: K4, p1, k20, p1, k15.

Row 13: Sl 1, k6, k2 tog, m2, sl 1, k1, psso, k9, k2 tog, m2, sl 1, k1, psso, k4, (m1, k2 tog) 3 times, m1, k7 (42 sts).

Row 14: Cast off 2 sts, k17, p1, k12, p1, k8 (40 sts).

Row 15: Sl 1, k2, m1, (k2 tog) twice, m2, (k2 tog) twice, m2, sl 1, k1, psso, k1, k2 tog, m2, (k2 tog) twice, m2, (k2 tog) twice, m2, sl 1, k1, psso, k3, (m1, k2 tog) 3 times, m1, k2, m2, k2 tog, k in f&b of last st (43 sts).

Row 16: K4, p1, k14, p1, (k3, p1) twice, k4, p1, k3, p1, k6.

Row 17: Sl 1, k6, k2 tog, m2, sl 1, k1, psso, k9, k2 tog, m2, sl 1, k1, psso, k6, (m1, k2 tog) 3 times, m1, k7 (44 sts).

Row 18: Cast off 2 sts, k19, p1, k12, p1, k8 (42 sts).

Row 19: Sl 1, k2, m1, (k2 tog) twice, m2, (k2 tog) twice, m2, sl 1, k1, psso, k1, k2 tog [m2, (k2 tog) twice] twice, m2, sl 1, k1, psso, k2, k2 tog, (m1, k2 tog) 4 times, k1, m2, k2 tog, k in f&b of last st (43 sts).

Row 20: K4, p1, k14, (p1, k3) twice, p1, k4, p1, k3, p1, k6 (43 sts).

Row 21: Sl 1, k6, k2 tog, m2, sl 1, k1, psso, k9, k2 tog, m2, sl 1, k1, psso, k3, k2 tog, (m1, k2 tog) 4 times, k6 (42 sts).

Row 22: Cast off 2 sts, k17, p1, k12, p1, k8 (40 sts).

Row 23: Sl 1, k2, m1, k2 tog, k9, k2 tog, m2, k2 tog, k8, k2 tog, (m1, k2 tog) 4 times, k1, m2, k2 tog, k in f&b of last st (41 sts).

Row 24: K4, p1, k20, p1, k15.

Row 25: Sl 1, k24, k2 tog (m1, k2 tog) 4 times, k6 (40 sts).

Row 26: Cast off 2 sts, k37 (38 sts).

Row 27: Sl 1, k2, m1, k2 tog, k9, k2 tog, m2, k2 tog, k6, k2 tog, (m1, k2 tog) 4 times, k1, m2, k2 tog, k in f&b in last st (39 sts).

Row 28: K4, p1, k18, p1, k15.

Row 29: Sl 1, k22, k2 tog, (m1, k2 tog) 4 times, k6 (38 sts).

Row 30: Cast off 2 sts, k35 (36 sts).

Row 31: Sl 1, k2, m1, k2 tog, k9, k2 tog, m2, k2 tog, k4, k2 tog, (m1, k2 tog) 4 times, k1, m2, k2 tog, k in f&b of last st (37 sts).

Row 32: K4, p1, k16, p1, k15.

Row 33: Sl 1, k5 (m1, k2 tog) 4 times, k5, k2 tog, (m1, k2 tog) 5 times, k6 (36 sts).

Row 34: Cast off 2 sts, k33 (34 sts).

Repeat rows 3–34 until length desired.

To make up

Pad the wood and insert hook in the centre of the hanger. Sew the 2 strips of knitting together leaving a space in the centre for the hook. Place knitting over the hanger. Thread ribbon through the bottom holes to link the cover together. Cover hook with ribbon or a knitted strip. Tie a ribbon bow at the base of the hook.

MACALIE

Cast on 20 sts.
Knit 1 row.

Row 1: Sl 1, k1, (m1, k2 tog, k1) 4 times, k2 tog, m2, k2 tog, k1, (m1, k1) 4 times in last st.

Row 2: Make a picot thus:
Cast on 2 sts on LH needle. K the 2 sts. Lift 1st st over 2nd. K one st from LH needle. Lift 1st st over 2nd, leaving 1 st on RH needle, k7, m1, k2tog, k1, p1, k1, (m1, k2 tog, k1) twice, m1, k2 tog, k6.

Row 3: Sl 1, k1, (m1, k2 tog, k1) 3 times, m1, k2 tog, k14.

Row 4: Make a picot: K7, m1, k2 tog, k3, (m1, k2 tog, k1) twice, m1, k2 tog, k6.

Row 5: Sl 1, k1, (m1, k2 tog, k1) 4 times, k2 tog, m2, k2 tog, k9.

Row 6: Make a picot: K7, m1, k2 tog, k1, p1, k1, (m1, k2 tog, k1) twice, m1, k2 tog, k6.

Row 7: Sl 1, k1, (m1, k2 tog, k1) 3 times, m1, k2 tog, k14.

Row 8: Make a picot: K7, m1, k2 tog, k3, (m1, k2 tog, k1) twice, m1, k2 tog, k6.

Row 9: Sl 1, k1, (m1, k2 tog, k1) 4 times, k2 tog, m2, k2 tog, k9.

Row 10: Make a picot: K7, m1, k2 tog, k1, p1, k1, (m1, k2 tog, k1) twice, m1, k2 tog, k6.

Row 11: Sl 1, k1, (m1, k2 tog, k1) 3 times, m1, k2 tog, k6. Lift the 7 sts over the st nearest the point of the needle, k1.

Row 12: Make a picot: K5, (m1, k2 tog, k1) twice, m1, k2 tog, k6 (20 sts).

Repeat rows 1–12 until length desired.
Make 2 strips of lace.
The width of the lace can be varied by adding or subtracting sts divisible by 3.

To make up

Pad the wood and insert hook in the centre of the hanger. Sew the 2 strips of knitting together leaving a space in the centre for the hook. Place knitting over the hanger. Thread ribbon through the bottom holes to link the cover together. Cover hook with ribbon or a knitted strip. Tie a ribbon bow at the base of the hook.

The towel

Make a length of lace to fit the towel and attach to towel with tiny sts. Add a motif or bow to the towel and thread with ribbons if desired.

JOAN

Cast on 35 sts.
Row 1: Knit.
Row 2: Sl 1, k2, (m1, k2 tog) twice, k2, (m1, k2 tog) 3 times, k2, m2, k2 tog, k16.
Row 3: M1, k2 tog, k16, p1, k17.
Row 4: Sl 1, k to end of row.
Row 5: M1, k2 tog, k to end of row.
Row 6: Sl 1, k2, (m1, k2 tog) twice, k2, (m1, k2 tog) 3 times, k2, (m2, k2 tog) twice, k15.
Row 7: M1, k2 tog, k15, p1, k2, p1, k17.
Row 8: Sl 1, k to end of row.
Row 9: M1, k2 tog, k to end of row.
Row 10: Sl 1, k2, (m1, k2 tog) twice, k2, (m1, k2 tog) 3 times, k2, (m2, k2 tog) 3 times, k15.
Row 11: M1, k2 tog, k15, p1, (k2, p1) twice, k17.
Row 12: Sl 1, k to end of row.
Row 13: M1, k2 tog, k to end of row.
Row 14: Sl 1, k2, (m1, k2 tog) twice, k2, (m1, k2 tog) 3 times, k2, (m2, k2 tog) 4 times, k16.

Row 15: M1, k2 tog, k16, (p1, k2) 3 times, p1, k17.
Row 16: Sl 1, k to end of row.
Row 17: M1, k2 tog, k to end of row.
Row 18: Sl 1, k2, (m1, k2 tog) twice, k2, (m1, k2 tog) 3 times, k2, (m2, k2 tog) 5 times, k18.
Row 19: M1, k2 tog, k18, (p1, k2) 4 times, p1, k17.
Row 20: Sl 1, k49.
Row 21: M1, k2 tog, k to end of row.
Row 22: Sl 1, k32, sl 15 sts over the next st, p1, k1.
Row 23: Sl 1, k to end of row.
Repeat rows 1–23 until length desired.

To make up

Pad the wood and insert hook in the centre of the hanger. Sew the 2 strips of knitting together leaving a space in the centre for the hook. Place knitting over the hanger. Thread ribbon through the bottom holes to link the cover together. Cover hook with ribbon or a knitted strip. Tie a ribbon bow at the base of the hook.

32: HEARTS AND FLOWERS

Heart shaped Hearts and Flowers aromatic sachets feature different laces and flowers on a basic heart motif. Together with the two square sachets, Parterre on the lower left and Sophie, upper right, these designs make a useful gift, ideal to use as protection for stored layettes. See pattern headings for materials used in Parterre and Sophie.

Materials

Heart motif: 1 × 50 g ball Anny Blatt Coton d'Egypte
Needles 3 mm (11)
Lace edgings: 1 × 20 g ball DMC Cebelia 10
Needles 2 mm (14)
Flowers: 1 × 20 g ball DMC 20
Needles 1.25 mm (18)
DMC embroidery yarn
Ribbon if desired

HEARTS AND FLOWERS

Sachet

Cast on 2 sts.
Row 1: Knit.

Continue in st, st inc both ends of every row until there are 22 sts on needle.
Row 12: Purl.
Row 13: Knit, inc both ends of row.
Row 14: Purl.
Row 15: Knit, inc both ends of row.
Work in st, st for 12 rows.
Row 28: Dec in next st, p9, p2 tog, sl 1, p1, psso, p9, dec in last st.
Row 29: Dec in next st, k9. Turn.
Continue on these 10 sts.
Row 30: Dec in next st, p6, dec in last st.
Row 31: Dec in next st, k4, dec in last st.
Row 32: Cast off.
Join yarn to remaining sts. Work other side to correspond.

To make up

Stitch sachet together, leaving 5 cm (2″) opening. Embroider, and trim as desired. Fill with padding and potpourri. Stitch the opening together and add lace edging of your choice, taking care to allow fullness around curves. Attach ribbons to hang sachet if desired.

Edging 1

Cast on 4 sts.
Row 1: K1, p3.
Row 2: K1, m1, k1 tbl, m1, sl 1, k1, psso.
Row 3: K1, p2, (k1, p1, k1, p1) in next st, p1.
Row 4: Cast off 4 sts, k1, m1, sl 1, k1, psso.
Repeat rows 1–4 until length desired.

Edging 2

Cast on 4 sts.
Row 1: Sl 1, k1, m2, k2.
Row 2: K3, p1, k2.
Row 3: Sl 1, k5.
Row 4: K6.
Row 5: Sl 1, k1, m2, k2 tog, m2, k2.
Row 6: K3, (p1, k2) twice.
Row 7: Sl 1, k8.
Row 8: Cast off 5 sts, k3.
Repeat rows 1–8 until length desired.

Edging 3

Cast on 4 sts.
Row 1: K1, m1, k2 tog, m2, k1.
Row 2: K2, p1, k1, m1, k2 tog.
Row 3: K1, m1, k2 tog, k3.
Row 4: Cast off 2 sts, k1, m1, k2 tog.
Repeat rows 1–4 until length desired.

Lace rosettes

Using fine thread and needles, cast on 4 sts.
Row 1: M1, k2 tog, k2.
Repeat this row 29 times.
Cast off, leaving long thread. Using fine needle thread through loops along edge of work. Draw up to form rosette. Fasten off.
Make a bullion stitch flower for the centre. Stitch rosette into position.

Miniature rose

Using fine thread and needles, cast on 10 sts.
Row 1: K1, * m1, k1 *, repeat *–* to end of row.
Repeat this row twice.
Cast off.
Arrange knitting to form a miniature rose.
Use as desired.

PARTERRE SQUARE SACHET

A lavender sachet from the nineteenth century, knitted by Barbara Hosking using DMC 20 cotton and size 1.25 mm (18) needles. Sachet is approximately 15 cm (6″) square.

Cast on 3 sts.
Next rows: M1, k to end of each row, working until you have 10 sts.
Proceed as follows:
Row 1: M1, k3, k2 tog, m1, k5.
Row 2 and all even rows: M1, k to end of row.
Row 3: M1, k3, k2 tog, m1, k1, m1, k2 tog, k4.
Row 5: M1, k3, k2 tog, m1, k3, m1, k2 tog, k4.
Row 7: M1, k3, k2 tog, m1, k5, m1, k2 tog, k4.
Row 9: M1, k3, k2 tog, m1, k2, k2 tog, m1, k3, m1, k2 tog, k4.
Row 11: M1, k3, k2 tog, m1, k2, k2 tog, m1, k1, m1, k2 tog, k2, m1, k2 tog, k4.
Row 13: M1, k3, k2 tog, m1, k2, k2 tog, m1, k3, m1, k2 tog, k2, m1, k2 tog, k4.
Row 15: M1, k3, k2 tog, m1, k2, k2 tog, m1, k5, m1, k2 tog, k2, m1, k2 tog, k4.
Row 17: M1, k3, k2 tog, m1, k2, k2 tog, m1, k2, k2 tog, m1, k3, m1, k2 tog, k2, m1, k2 tog, k4.
Row 19: M1, k3, k2 tog, m1, k2, k2 tog, m1, k2, k2 tog, m1, k1, m1, k2 tog, k2, m1, k2 tog, k2, m1, k2 tog, k4.
Row 21: M1, k3, k2 tog, m1, k2, k2 tog, m1, k2, k2 tog, m1, k3, m1, k2 tog, k2, m1, k2 tog, k2, m1, k2 tog, k4.
Row 23: M1, k3, k2 tog, m1, k2, k2 tog, m1, k2, k2 tog, m1, k5, (m1, k2 tog, k2) twice, m1, k2 tog, k4.
Row 25: M1, k3, (k2 tog, m1, k2) twice, k2 tog, m1, k7, (m1, k2 tog, k2) twice, m1, k2 tog, k4.
Row 27: M1, k3, (k2 tog, m1, k2) twice, k2 tog, m1, k3, k2 tog, m2, k4, (m1, k2 tog, k2) twice, m1, k2 tog, k4.
Row 29: M1, k3, (k2 tog, m1, k2) 3 times, k2 tog, m2, (k2 tog) twice, m2, (k2 tog, k2, m1) 3 times, k2 tog, k4.
Row 31: M1, k3, (k2 tog, m1, k2) twice, k2 tog, m1, k5, k2 tog, m2, k2 tog, k5, m1, (k2 tog, k2, m1) twice, k2 tog, k4.

Row 33: M1, k3, k2 tog, m1, k2, k2 tog, m1, k1, m1, k2 tog, k2, m1, k2 tog, k1, k2 tog, m2, (k2 tog) twice, m2, k2 tog, k1, k2 tog, m1, k2, k2 tog, m1, k1, m1, k2 tog, k2, m1, k2 tog, k4.

Row 35: M1, k3, k2 tog, m1, k2, k2 tog, m1, k3, (m1, k2 tog, k2) twice, k2 tog, m2, k2 tog, (k2, k2 tog, m1) twice, k3, m1, k2 tog, k2, m1, k2 tog, k4.

Row 37: M1, k3, k2 tog, m1, k2, k2 tog, m1, k5, m1, k2 tog, k2, m1, k2 tog, k6, k2 tog, m1, k2, k2 tog, m1, k5, m1, k2 tog, k2, m1, k2 tog, k4.

Row 39: M1, k3, (k2 tog, m1, k2) twice, k2 tog, m1, k3, m1, k2 tog, k2, m1, k2 tog, k4, (k2 tog, m1, k2) twice, k2 tog, m1, k3, m1, k2 tog, k2, m1, k2 tog, k4.

Row 41: M1, k3, (k2 tog, m1, k2) twice, k2 tog, m1, k1, (m1, k2 tog, k2) 3 times, (k2 tog, m1, k2) twice, k2 tog, m1, k1, (m1, k2 tog, k2) twice, m1, k2 tog, k4.

Row 43: M1, k3, (k2 tog, m1, k2) twice, k2 tog, m1, k3, (m1, k2 tog, k2) twice, m1, (k2 tog) twice. Pull one st over m1, (k2, k2 tog, m1) twice, k3, (m1, k2 tog, k2) twice, m1, k2 tog, k4.

Row 45: M1, k3, (k2 tog, m1, k2) twice, k2 tog, m1, k5, m1, k2 tog, k2, m1, k2 tog, k5, k2 tog, m1, k2, k2 tog, m1, k5, (m1, k2 tog, k2) twice, m1, k2 tog, k4.

Row 47: M1, k3, (k2 tog, m1, k2) twice, k2 tog, m1, k7, m1, k2 tog, k2, m1, k2 tog, k3, k2 tog, m1, k2, k2 tog, m1, k7, (m1, k2 tog, k2) twice, m1, k2 tog, k4.

Row 49: M1, k3, (k2 tog, m1, k2) twice, k2 tog, m1, k3, k2 tog, m2, k4, m1, k2 tog, k2, m1, k2 tog, k1, k2 tog, m1, k2, k2 tog, m1, k3, k2 tog, m2, k4, (m1, k2 tog, k2) twice, m1, k2 tog, k4.

Row 51: M1, k3, (k2 tog, m1, k2) 3 times, k2 tog, m2, (k2 tog) twice, m2, (k2 tog, k2, m1) twice, k3 tog, (m1, k2, k2 tog) twice, m2, (k2 tog) twice, m2, (k2 tog, k2, m1) 3 times, k2 tog, k4.

Row 53: M1, k3, (k2 tog, m1, k2) twice, k2 tog, m1, k5, k2 tog, m2, k2 tog, k5, m1, k2 tog, k5, k2 tog, m1, k5, k2 tog, m2, k2 tog, k5, (m1, k2 tog, k2) twice, m1, k2 tog, k4.

Row 54: M1, k to end of row.
There are now 66 sts on the needle.

Row 55: M1, (k2 tog) twice, (k2, m1, k2 tog) 3 times, k1, k2 tog, m2, (k2 tog) twice, m2, k2 tog, k1, k2 tog, m1, k2, k2 tog, m1, k1, m1, k2 tog, k2, m1, k2 tog, k1, k2 tog, m2, (k2 tog) twice, m2, k2 tog, k1, (k2 tog, m1, k2) twice, k2 tog, m1, k2 tog, k5.

Row 56 and all even rows: Decrease as follows: M1, k2 tog, k to end of row.

Row 57: M1, (k2 tog) twice, (k2, m1, k2 tog) 3 times, k2, k2 tog, m2, k2 tog, (k2, k2 tog, m1) twice, k3, (m1, k2 tog, k2) twice, k2 tog, m2, k2 tog, (k2, k2 tog, m1) 3 times, k2, (k2 tog) twice, k1.

Row 59: M1, (k2 tog) twice, (k2, m1, k2 tog) 3 times, k6, k2 tog, m1, k2, k2 tog, m1, k5, m1, k2 tog, k2, m1, k2 tog, k6, (k2 tog, m1, k2) 3 times, k2 tog, k2.

Row 61: M1, (k2 tog) twice, (k2, m1, k2 tog) 3 times, k4, (k2 tog, m1, k2) twice, k2 tog, m1, k3, m1, k2 tog, k2, m1, k2 tog, k4, (k2 tog, m1, k2) 3 times, k2 tog, k2.

Row 63: M1, (k2 tog) twice, (k2, m1, k2 tog) 3 times, (k2, k2 tog, m1) 3 times, k1, (m1, k2 tog, k2) 3 times, (k2 tog, m1, k2) 3 times, k2 tog, k2.

Row 65: M1, (k2 tog) twice, (k2, m1, k2 tog) 3 times, k2 tog. Pull one st over, (m1, k2, k2 tog) twice, m1, k3, m1, (k2 tog, k2, m1) twice, (k2 tog) twice. Pull one st over, (m1, k2, k2 tog) 3 times, k2.

Row 67: M1, (k2 tog) twice, (k2, m1, k2 tog) twice, k5, k2 tog, m1, k2, k2 tog, m1, k5, m1, k2 tog, k2, m1, k2 tog, k5, (k2 tog, m1, k2) twice, k2 tog, k2.

Row 69: M1, (k2 tog) twice, (k2, m1, k2 tog) twice, k3, (k2 tog) twice, m1, k2, k2 tog, m1, k7, m1, k2 tog, k2, m1, k2 tog, k3, (k2 tog, m1, k2) twice, k2 tog, k2.

Row 71: M1, (k2 tog) twice, (k2, m1, k2 tog) twice, k1, k2 tog, m1, k2, k2 tog, m1, k3, k2 tog, m2, k4, m1, k2 tog, k2, m1, k2 tog, k1, (k2 tog, m1, k2) twice, k2 tog, k2.

Row 73: M1, (k2 tog) twice, k2, m1, k2 tog, k2, m1, k3 tog, (m1, k2, k2 tog) twice, m2, (k2 tog) twice, m2, (k2 tog, k2, m1) twice, k3 tog, (m1, k2, k2 tog) twice, k2.

Row 75: M1, (k2 tog) twice, k2, m1, k2 tog, k5, k2 tog, m1, k5, k2 tog, m2, k2 tog, k5, m1, k2 tog, k5, k2 tog, m1, k2, k2 tog, k2.

Row 77: M1, (k2 tog) twice, (k2, m1, k2 tog) 3 times, k1, k2 tog, m2, (k2 tog) twice, m2, k2 tog, k1, (k2 tog, m1, k2) 3 times, k2 tog, k2.

Row 79: M1, (k2 tog) twice, (k2, m1, k2 tog) 3 times, k2, k2 tog, m2, k2 tog, (k2, k2 tog, m1) 3 times, k2, k2 tog, k2.

Row 81: M1, (k2 tog) twice, (k2, m1, k2 tog) 3 times, k6, (k2 tog, m1, k2) 3 times, k2 tog, k2.

Row 83: M1, (k2 tog) twice, (k2, m1, k2 tog) 3 times, k4, (k2 tog, m1, k2) 3 times, k2 tog, k2.

Row 85: M1, (k2 tog) twice, (k2, m1, k2 tog) 3 times, (k2, k2 tog, m1) 3 times, k2, k2 tog, k2.

Row 87: M1, (k2 tog) twice, (k2, m1, k2 tog) 3 times, k2 tog. Pull one st over, (m1, k2, k2 tog) 3 times, k2.

Row 89: M1, (k2 tog) twice, (k2, m1, k2 tog) twice, k5, (k2 tog, m1, k2) twice, k2 tog, k2.

Row 91: M1, (k2 tog) twice, (k2, m1, k2 tog) twice, k3, (k2 tog, m1, k2) twice, k2 tog, k2.

Row 93: M1, (k2 tog) twice, (k2, m1, k2 tog) twice, k1, (k2 tog, m1, k2) twice, k2 tog, k2.

Row 95: M1, (k2 tog) twice, k2, m1, k2 tog, k2, m1, k3 tog, (m1, k2, k2 tog) twice, k2.

Row 97: M1, (k2 tog) twice, k2, m1, k2 tog, k5, k2 tog, m1, k2, k2 tog, k2.

Row 99: M1, (k2 tog) twice, k2, m1, k2 tog, k3, k2 tog, m1, k2, k2 tog, k2.

Row 101: M1, (k2 tog) twice, k2, m1, k2 tog, k1, k2 tog, m1, k2, k2 tog, k2.

Row 103: M1, (k2 tog) twice, k2, m1, k3 tog, m1, k2, k2 tog, k2.

Row 105: M1, (k2 tog) twice, k5, k2 tog, k2.
Row 107: M1, (k2 tog) twice, k3, k2 tog, k2.
Row 109: M1, (k2 tog) twice, k1, k2 tog, k2.
Row 111: M1, (k2 tog) 3 times, k1.
Row 113: M1, (k2 tog) twice, k1.
Row 115: M1, (k2 tog) twice.
Cast off.

Edging

Cast on 13 sts.
Row 1: ** Sl 1, k2, k2 tog, m1, k1, m1, k2 tog, k1, m1, k2 tog, m1, k2.
Row 2 and alternate rows:: Knit.
Row 3: Sl 1, k1, k2 tog, m1, k3, m1, k2 tog, k1, m1, k2 tog, m1, k2.
Row 5: Sl 1, k2 tog, m1, k5, m1, k2 tog, k1, m1, k2 tog, m1, k2.
Row 7: Sl 1, k2, m1, k2 tog, k1, k2 tog, m1, k4, m1, k2 tog, m1, k2.
Row 9: Sl 1, k3, m1, k3 tog, m1, k6, m1, k2 tog, m1, k2.
Row 11: Knit.
Row 12: Cast off 5 sts, k12.
Repeat rows 1–12, 6 times.

Commence corner:
Row 1: Sl 1, k8, m1, k2 tog, m1, k2.
Row 2: K12, turn, leaving 2 sts on needle.
Row 3: Sl 1, k2, k2 tog, m2, k2 tog, k1, m1, k2 tog, m1, k2.
Row 4: K8, p1, k2, turn, leaving 4 sts on needle.
Row 5: Sl 1, k6, m1, k2 tog, m1, k2.
Row 6: K10, turn, leaving 6 sts on needle.
Row 7: Sl 1, k5, m1, k2 tog, m1, k2.
Row 8: K9, turn, leaving 8 sts on needle.
Row 9: Sl 1, k4, m1, k2 tog, m1, k2.
Row 10: K8, turn leaving 10 sts on needle.
Row 11: Sl 1, k7.
Row 12: Cast off 5 sts, k12.
Repeat rows 1–12, 4 times **.
This completes one side and corner of edging. Repeat **–** 3 times.
Sew edging to sachet, taking care to place point of square in centre of corner. Make a fabric square of fine material, approx. 9 cm (3½"). Fill with lavender or potpourri. Attach knitted square at the corners with tiny sts.
Place a silk ribbon bow in each corner. Knitted top can be removed for laundering and perfumed pad easily replaced. A separate knitted square could replace fabric if desired.

SOPHIE

Made by Betty Featherstone from a nineteenth century pincushion pattern.

Materials

1 ball DMC 20 cotton
Needles 1.25 mm (18)
Narrow ribbon for 4 small bows
DMC stranded cotton for embroidery
Fibrefill

Front

Cast on 45 sts. Work in moss st.
Row 1: K1, (p1, k1) to end of row.
Repeat row 1, 23 times.
Row 25: Moss st 15, k15, moss st 15.
Row 26: Moss st 15, p15, moss st 15.
Repeat rows 25 and 26, 11 times.
Repeat row 1, 24 times (moss st).
Cast off.

Back

Cast on 45 sts.
Row 1: K1, (p1, k1). Repeat to end of row.
Repeat row 1, 71 times.
Cast off.

Edging

Cast on 8 sts.
Row 1: Sl 1, k1, m1, k2 tog, k1, m2, k2 tog, k1.
Row 2: K3, p1, k2, m1, k2 tog, k1.
Row 3: Sl 1, k1, m1, k2 tog, k2, m2, k2 tog, k1.
Row 4: K3, p1, k3, m1, k2 tog, k1.
Row 5: Sl 1, k1, m1, k2 tog, k3, m2, k2 tog, k1.
Row 6: K3, p1, k4, m1, k2 tog, k1.
Row 7: Sl 1, k1, m1, k2 tog, k7.
Row 8: Cast off 3 sts, k4, m1, k2 tog, k1.
Repeat rows 1–8 until length required to trim cushion, allowing fullness at the corners. Sew back and front together on 3 sides. Insert potpourri mixed with fibrefill. Stitch the 4th side. Sew edging around the cushion. Attach 4 small bows at corners. Embroider rosebuds with tiny leaves. The plain square in the centre is an ideal spot for an initial or monogram.

33: MY BEARS

Illustrated on page 106.

Materials

A small quantity of cotton for each bear

Height	Cotton	Needles
6.25 cm (2½″)	DMC 8	1.25 mm (18)
7.5 cm (3″)	DMC 20	1.25 mm (18)
12.75 cm (5″)	4-ply	1.5 mm (16)
16 cm (6¼″)	4-ply	2 mm (14)

DMC stranded cotton for embroidering features and flowers
Small amount of dacron filling
Narrow ribbon for neck

MY BEAR

Ears (make 2)

Cast on 8 sts.
Knit 2 rows.
K2 tog each end of the next 2 rows.
Cast off for single ears.
Proceed as follows for double ears: Inc 1 st at each end of the next 2 rows.
Knit 2 rows.
Cast off.
Fold ears, joining cast-on and cast-off edges. Shape ears into a gentle curve with your fingers.

Head

Cast on 12 sts.
Knit 1 row.
Next row: K1, (k in f&b of each st until last st), k1 (22 sts).
Knit 4 rows.
Next row: K6, inc 1, k1, inc 1, k8, inc 1, k1, inc 1, k6.
Knit 3 rows.
Next row: K7, inc 1, k1, inc 1, k10, inc 1, k1, inc 1, k7.
Knit 3 rows.
Next row: K1, (k2 tog) to last st, k1.
Knit 3 rows.

Next row: K2 tog, k3, (sl 1, k2 tog, psso) twice, k3, k2 tog.
Knit 1 row.
Next row: (K2 tog) to end of row (5 sts).
Cut yarn and thread through remaining sts to form crown of head.

Body

Cast on 14 sts.
Knit 1 row.
Next row: K1, (k in f&b of each st until last st), k1 (26 sts).
Knit 3 rows.
Next row: K7, inc 1, k11, inc 1, k8 (28 sts).
Knit 5 rows.
Next row: K7, inc 1, k13, inc 1, k8 (30 sts).
Knit 6 rows (adjust body length here if desired).
Next row: K7, k2 tog, k13, k2 tog, k6.
Knit 2 rows.
Next row: (K2 tog) to end of row (14 sts).
Next row: (K2 tog) to end of row (7 sts).
Cut yarn and thread through remaining sts at neck edge.
Fasten off securely.

Legs (make 2)

Cast on 10 sts.
Knit 1 row.
Next row: K1, (k in f&b of each st until last st), k1 (18 sts).
Knit 3 rows.
Next row: Shape paw thus:
K4, k2 tog, (Sl 1, k2 tog, psso) twice, k2 tog, k4.
Next row: Knit.
Next row: Knit, inc 1 st at each end of the row (14 sts).
Knit 7 rows. Adjust leg length here if desired.
Next row: (K2 tog) to end of row (7 sts).
Knit 1 row.
Cut yarn and thread through remaining sts at top of leg.
Fasten off securely.

Arms (make 2)

Cast on 7 sts.
Knit 1 row.
Next row: K1, (k in f&b of each st until last st), k1, (12 sts).
Knit 9 rows. Adjust arm length here if desired.
Next row: K3, (k2 tog) to last 3 sts, k3.

Nine My Bears of different sizes frolic in a lavender copse, accompanied by Lavinia Lavender, with Lavender Pomanders and a Lavender Semicircle in the foreground. All nine bears, varying in height from 6.25 cm to 16 cm (2½" to 6¼") are knitted from the My Bear pattern using different sizes of cotton and needles. Directions for Lavender Semicircle appear on page 112.

Knit 3 rows.
Next row: K1, (k2 tog) to end of row (5 sts).
Cut yarn and thread through remaining sts at paw. Fasten off securely.

Assembling the bear

Stitch seams of head, body, legs and arms (cast-on edges are left open to facilitate stuffing).
Insert small quantity of filling into each section until firm, then run a thread through each opening. Draw together tightly and fasten securely. A small amount of lavender enclosed in muslin can be inserted in the torso of the bear, making an aromatic gift for an arctophile. Attach limbs to torso, making each one secure. Fold and stitch double ears, shape ears with fingers to form curve. Stitch into position. Embroider the eyes and muzzle of the bear in the colour of your choice using DMC stranded cotton. Touches of embroidery scattered at random over the bear give a pleasant effect. Complete the bear with a ribbon bow at the neck.
Note: Omit lavender filling if the bear is a gift for a child, or if it is to receive constant laundering.

LAVINIA LAVENDER

Height: 22 cm (8¾")
Begin at the head.
Cast on 12 sts.
Row 1: Knit.
Row 2: Inc both ends of row (14 sts).
Row 3: Purl.
Repeat rows 2 and 3, twice (18 sts).
Row 8: Knit 10 rows.
Row 18: (K2 tog) both ends of row (16 sts).
Row 19: Purl.
Repeat rows 18–19 once (14 sts).
Row 22: Knit, inc both ends of row (16 sts).
Row 23: Knit.
Repeat rows 22–23 twice (20 sts).
Row 28: Cast on 2 sts, knit (22 sts).
Repeat row 28 (24 sts).
Row 30: Knit 30 rows.
Row 60: K12, leave remaining 12 sts on spare needle.
Row 61: Knit 23 rows.

Row 84: (K2 tog) both ends of row (10 sts).
Row 85: Knit.
Repeat rows 84–85 once (8 sts).
Knit 20 rows.
Row 108: (K2 tog) both ends of needle (6 sts).
Row 109: Cast off.
Knit other leg in same manner.

Arms (make 2)

Cast on 3 sts.
Row 1: Knit.
Row 2: Inc in first and third sts (5 sts).
Row 3: Knit.
Repeat rows 2–3, 5 times (15 sts).
Row 14: Knit 22 rows.
Row 36: (K2 tog) both ends of needle (13 sts).
Repeat row 36, 3 times (7 sts).
Cast off.

Beret

Cast on 30 sts.
Row 1: Knit.
Row 2: (K1, p1) to end of row.
Repeat row 2, 4 times.
Row 7: Inc in every 2nd st (45 sts).
Row 8: Knit.
Repeat rows 7–8 once (68 sts).
Row 11: Knit 12 rows.
Row 23: (K2 tog) 12 times at even distances along row (56 sts).
Row 24: Knit.
Repeat rows 23–24, 3 times (20 sts).
Cut the yarn and thread through sts. Draw up tightly. Sew seam of beret, darn a length of silk ribbon above ribbing, tie at side as illustrated.

Assembling Lavinia

Sew the seams, leaving an opening at one side for stuffing. Turn the knitting the right side out. Stuff with filling. Sew up the opening. Sew arms, stuff and sew onto doll. Embroider features. Wind small quantity of No. 8 DMC perle cotton around fingers to form hair. Stitch to head. Place beret over hair and stitch into place.

DRESS

Cast on 80 sts.
Knit 4 rows.
With right side facing, work 26 rows st, st.
Next row: (K2 tog) to end of row (40 sts).
Purl 1 row.
Cast off.

Bodice

Cast on 44 sts.
Work 4 rows st, st.
Divide sts.
Knit 12 sts for left side leaving 32 sts on holder.
Knit 22 rows. Cast off.
Pick up 20 sts from holder for front of dress, working 16 rows st, st.

Shape neck:
K8, cast off 4 sts, k8.
Continue on 8 sts.
Purl one row.
Next row: K2 tog, k to end of row (7 sts).
Work 3 rows.
Cast off.
Work other side to correspond, reversing shaping. Join yarn to remaining 12 sts.
Work 16 rows.
Cast off.

Sleeves:
Cast on 16 sts.
Knit 2 rows.
Next row: K1, (k2 tog, m1) to end of row.
Work 6 rows.
Cast off.

To make up dress

Sew skirt seam and attach bodice to skirt (leaving 2 sts overlap at centre back). Close opening with press studs. Sew sleeve seams and insert into armholes. Knit sufficient Lavender Lace edging to trim hem of dress. Knit a length of Underlace and attach inside dress on garter st ridge.
Lavinia wears a white embroidered collar. A length of lace could be sewn around neck of dress if desired.

LAVENDER LACE EDGING

Cast on 4 sts.
Row 1: K1, p3.
Row 2: K1, m1, k1 tbl, m1, sl 1, k1, psso.
Row 3: K1, p2, (k1, p1, k1, p1) into next st, p1.
Row 4: Cast off 4 sts, k1, m1, sl 1, k1, psso.
Repeat rows 1–4 until length required.

DOLL UNDERLACE

Cast on 9 sts.
Row 1: K9.
Row 2: M1, k3, m1, k2 tog, k4.
Row 3: K10.
Row 4: M1, k5, m1, k2 tog, k3.
Row 5: K11.
Row 6: M1, k3 tog, k1, k2 tog, m1, k5.
Row 7: K8, k2 tog.
Row 8: M1, k3 tog, m1, k6.
Repeat rows 1–8 until length desired.

LAVENDER POMANDERS

Cast on 40 sts.
Row 1: Knit to last st, turn.
Row 2: Sl 1, k to last st, turn.
Row 3 and 4: K to last 2 sts, turn.
Row 5 and 6: K to last 3 sts, turn.
Continue working this way until 10 sts remain at end and beginning of row. K to end of row. Repeat until 8 sections are completed.
Cast off.
Fill the ball with soft fibre to which you have added a spoonful of lavender flowers. Sew seam as neatly as possible. Decorate with knitted roses, embroidered lavender flowers or ribbons.

34: CHRISTENING CAKE FRILL

Ruth Rintoule's design for a christening cake frill will become a family treasure; it would also make dainty tiebacks for the nursery curtains.

Insertion

Cast on 12 sts.
Row 1: K2, m1, (k2 tog) twice, m2, k2 tog, k2, m1, k2 tog.
Row 2: K2, m1, k2 tog, k2, p1, k3, m1, k2 tog.
Rows 3 and 4: K2, m1, k2 tog, k6, m1, k2 tog.
Repeat rows 1–4 until length desired.

Narrow lace

Cast on 5 sts.
Row 1: K2, m1, k1, m1, k2.
Row 2: Knit.
Row 3: K3, m1, k2 tog, m1, k2.
Row 4: Knit.
Row 5: K4, m1, k2 tog, m1, k2.
Row 6: Cast off 4 sts, k to end of row.
Repeat rows 1–6 until length required to edge insertion on both sides. Cast off. Thread ribbon through holes and sew to insertion.
For a wider frill, use two pieces of insertion and slip stitch together.

35: THE TRAVELLERS

This collection features two versions of the Bear Cosy to cover bottles of different sizes. At centre front is a Lavender Circle pincushion, behind it a drink cover made from the same pattern. The tiny bear, Ursula, can be put to a variety of uses. The bears are wearing bow ties designed by Joan Eckersley—the large one is Edward, the small one Albert. All of these can be knitted in the yarn of your choice.

Measurements

Large bear cosy 17.5 cm (7")
Little bear cosy 10 cm (4")
Ursula (tiny bear) 6.5 cm (2½")

BEAR COSY

These covers are fun to knit and make a delightful gift for a baby.

Materials

Large bear: 8-ply cotton
Set of 4 needles 3.25 mm (10)
Little bear: 4-ply cotton
Set of 4 needles 2 mm (14)
Silk ribbon
DMC stranded cotton for embroidery
Soft filling for head and arms

Cast on 45 sts (15 sts on each of 3 needles). Work with 4th needle.
Purl 3 rounds.
Round 4: * K2 tog, k5, m1, k1, m1, k5, k2 tog. Repeat from * twice.
Round 5: Knit.
Repeat rounds 4 and 5, 14 times.
Round 34: * K1, k2 tog *. Repeat *–* 14 times.
Purl 3 rounds.
Round 38: Knit.
Round 39: * K1, p1 *. Repeat *–* 14 times.
Repeat round 39, 11 times.
Next round: K2 tog to end of round (15 sts).
Cut yarn. Thread through sts. Draw up to close top of head.
Fasten off on wrong side.

Arms (make 2)

Cast on 7 sts. Purl 1 row.
Next row: K1, (k in f&b of each st until last st), k1 (12 sts).
Beginning with purl row work 9 rows st, st.

Next row: K3, (sl 1, k1, psso) 4 times, k3 (10 sts).
Beginning with purl row work 3 rows st, st.
Next row: K1, (k2 tog) 4 times (5 sts).
Cut yarn and thread through remaining sts at paw. Fasten off securely.

Ears (make 2)

Cast on 8 sts, working on smaller needles.
Knit 2 rows.
K2 tog at each end of next 2 rows.
Cast off.

Lace collar

Cast on 4 sts.
Row 1: Sl 1, k1, m2, k2.
Row 2: K3, p1, k2.
Row 3: Sl 1, k5.
Row 4: K6.
Row 5: Sl 1, k1, m2, k2 tog, m2, k2.
Row 6: K3, (p1, k2) twice.
Row 7: Sl 1, k8.
Row 8: Cast off 5 sts, k3.
Repeat rows 1–8, 6 times or length desired.
Cast off.

To make up

Sew up arms and firmly stuff head and arms with fibre filling. Thread length of fine strong thread through sts on the first row of ribbing (round 39 of pattern). Draw together to form neck. Fasten thread securely.
Attach ears and arms to bear. Arrange and fasten collar around neck. Embroider features. Decorate with a touch of silk ribbon embroidery at hemline and with bow at neck.
The bottom of the bear is designed to remain open so that it can be used as a cover for a feeding bottle or talcum container. The little bear would be useful to cover a spare teat or a nosedrop bottle.

LAVENDER CIRCLES

Three different ways to use the circles knitted by Ruth Tyrie. They are finished with knobs made from the My Bear head pattern on page 105.

Materials

1 × 50 g ball DMC 20 cotton
Needles 2 mm (14)
Dacron filling for pincushion, bear heads
2 circles fine cotton, 15 cm (6″) diameter
Lavender
Narrow ribbon
Circle measures approx 16.5 cm (6½″) diameter

Cast on 25 sts.
Row 1: Sl 1, k19, m1, p2 tog, k1, m1, k2.
Row 2: K4, m1, p2 tog, k18, turn.
Row 3: Sl 1, k17, m1, p2 tog, k2, m1, k2.
Row 4: K5, m1, p2 tog, k16, turn.
Row 5: Sl 1, k15, m1, p2 tog, k3, m1, k2.
Row 6: K6, m1, p2 tog, k14, turn.
Row 7: Sl 1, k13, m1, p2 tog, k2 tog, m2, k2, m1, k2.
Row 8: K6, p1, k1, m1, p2 tog, k12, turn.
Row 9: Sl 1, k11, m1, p2 tog, k8.
Row 10: Cast off 5 sts, k2, p2 tog, k10, turn.
Row 11: Sl 1, k9, m1, p2 tog, k1, m1, k2.
Row 12: K4, m1, p2 tog, k8, turn.
Row 13: Sl 1, k7, m1, p2 tog, k2, m1, k2.
Row 14: K5, m1, p2 tog, k6, turn.
Row 15: Sl 1, k5, m1, p2 tog, k3, m1, k2.
Row 16: K6, m1, p2 tog, k4, turn.
Row 17: Sl 1, k3, m1, p2 tog, k2 tog, m2, k2, m1, k2.
Row 18: K6, p1, k1, m1, p2 tog, k2, turn.
Row 19: Sl 1, k1, m1, p2 tog, k8.
Row 20: Cast off 5 sts, k2, m1, p2 tog, k2, (m1, k2 tog) 8 times, k2.
Repeat rows 1–20 until work forms circle.

To make up

Join or graft seam of circle. Press lightly to form circle.

The pincushion or lavender cushion

Knit 2 complete circles. Cut two 15 cm (6″) circles from a fine cotton fabric. Stitch around circle leaving opening for filling. Fill with lavender flowers and dacron filling. Stitch opening neatly. Place lavender circle between the two knitted circles. Thread needle with fine ribbon and thread through holes of top and bottom knitted circles, joining the two circles. Decorate with bows. Knit and embroider My Bear head (page 105).

Attach to centre of circle as a knob. Thread needle with fine ribbon and thread through second circle of holes. Tie into bow. The ribbons are easily removed for replacing the lavender circle and laundering.
This little cushion would also make an attractive lid for a box or small basket. One complete circle can be folded in half to make an attractive semicircular sachet. Simply stitch through the two rows of holes near lace edging and at centre. Tie into a bow. You will need to make a semicircular lavender sachet to insert in circle of knitting. Another use for this knitted circle is a simple jug or drink cover for the nursery. Attach glass beads to each point of the lace. Make a My Bear head and attach as knob. Any knitted circle can be utilised in this way.

URSULA

A small bear approximately 6.5 cm (2½″) high. These tiny bears can be used as blind-pulls, pram toys and mobiles.

Materials

Small quantity 4-ply cotton
2 mm (14) needles
Length of narrow ribbon to tie around neck

Ears (make 2)

Cast on 4 sts.
Knit 2 rows.
Next row: K2 tog, k2 tog tbl.
Next row: K2 tog.
Cast off.

Head and body (in one piece)

Cast on 5 sts.
Knit one row.
Next row: K twice in every st (10 sts).
Next row: Knit.
Next row: K twice in every st (20 sts).
Knit 9 rows.
Next row: ** K2 tog to end of row.
Next row: Knit ** (10 sts).
Next row: Knit.
Next row: K twice in every st (20 sts).
Knit 5 rows.
Repeat **–** twice (5 sts).
Cut yarn and thread through remaining sts.

Arms (make 2)

Cast on 7 sts.
Next row: Knit, inc both ends of the row (9 sts).
Knit 8 rows.
Next row: K1, (k2 tog) to end of row.
Cut yarn and thread through remaining sts.

Legs (make 2)

Cast on 10 sts.
Knit 8 rows.
Next row: K2 tog to end of row (5 sts).
Cut yarn and thread through remaining sts.

To make up

Join body and head seam. Insert filling and close opening. Attach ears, embroider eyes, nose and mouth. Join arm and leg seams. Insert filling and close openings. Attach limbs to torso, stitching firmly. Tie ribbon bow around bear's neck.

ALBERT BOW TIE

Cast on 14 sts.
Knit one row.
Row 1: Sl 1, k2, p8, k3.
Row 2: Sl 1, k2, * (k1, p1, k1) in next st, p3 tog *. Repeat *–* once, k3.
Row 3: Sl 1, k2, p8, k3.
Row 4: Sl 1, k2, * p3 tog, (k1, p1, k1) in next st *. Repeat *–* once, k3.
Row 5: Sl 1, k2, p8, k3.
Repeat rows 2–5 until length desired.

Assembling the bow

For a 7 cm (2¾″) bow knit a 14 cm (5½″) strip. Sew ends together at centre back. Tie a piece of thread in the centre to form bow. Knit 6 or 8 rows of pattern. Cast off. Fold over bow.

 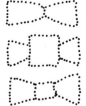

Neck band

Cast on 5 sts.
Row 1: Sl 1, k4.
Repeat until length desired.
Sew onto bow. Stitch press stud at the ends.

EDWARD BOW TIE

Cast on 19 sts.
Knit 4 rows.
Row 5: Sl 1, k2, (m1, k2 tog) 3 times, k2, (m1, k2 tog) 3 times, k2.
Row 6: Sl 1, k18.
Rows 7,9,11: As row 5.
Rows 8,10,12: As row 6.
Repeat rows 1–12 until length desired.

Neck band

Cast on 6 sts.
Knit 10 rows.
Row 1: Sl 1, k1, m1, k2 tog, k2.
Row 2: Sl 1, k5.
Row 3: Sl 1, k2, m1, k2 tog, k1.
Row 4: Sl 1, k5.
Repeat rows 1–4 until length desired ending with 10 knit rows.
Assemble as for Albert.

36: THEODORE

A bear knitted in one piece by Thea Moore. The pattern starts with the legs, continues with body and arms, then head (front and back), finally arms, body and legs — simple and effective.
Your choice of yarn and needles will determine the size of your bear. Thea used 100 g 8-ply cotton and 3.75 mm (9) needles. This Theodore is 30 cm (11¾") tall. (David Moore collection.)

Materials
100 g 8-ply cotton
Needles 3.75 mm (9)
DMC embroidery thread for face
Stuffing
Ribbon

Legs
** Cast on 12 sts. Knit 30 rows **, leave the 12 sts on st holder. Repeat from **–**, then work across both sets of sts to join legs.

Body
Knit 30 rows.

Arms
Cast on 15 sts at beginning of next 2 rows. Work 18 rows.
Cast off 15 sts at beginning of next 2 rows.

Head (front and back)
Knit 60 rows.

Arms
Cast on 15 sts at beginning of next 2 rows.
Work 18 rows.
Cast off 15 sts at beginning of next 2 rows.

Body
Knit 30 rows.

Legs
Knit 12 sts, turn (leaving remaining sts on st holder).
Knit 29 rows.
Cast off. Join yarn to remaining sts. Work the other leg to correspond.

To make up
Fold work in half, right sides together. Sew head, arms and side seams and across bottoms of legs, leaving inside leg seam open to facilitate stuffing. Turn right side out. St across corners for the ears (working approximately 5 rows down from the corner). Embroider Theodore's features. Fill the bear and close opening. Tie ribbon around neck.

37: THE GATHERING

Illustrated on page 116.

Materials

All collars are knitted in 4-ply cotton on 2 mm (14) needles

SELINARCTOS

Cast on 20 sts.

Knit 1 row.

Row 1: Sl 1, k5, m1, k2 tog, k2, m2, k2 tog, k1, turn (leaving remaining sts on needle).

Row 2: Sl 1, k2, m1, k2 tog, k5, m2, k2 tog, k2.

Row 3: Sl 1, k3, m1, k2 tog, k1, m1, k2 tog, k4, m2, k2 tog, k1, turn.

Row 4: Sl 1, k2, m1, k2 tog, k9, m2, k2 tog, k1.

Row 5: Sl 1, k2, m1, k2 tog, k3, m1, k2 tog, k6, m2, k2 tog, k1, turn.

Row 6: Sl 1, k2, m1, k2 tog, k15.

Row 7: Cast off 2 sts, k5 (not counting st on needle after cast-off), m1, k2 tog, k2, m2, k2 tog, k4, m2, k2 tog, k1, turn.

Row 8: Sl 1, k2, m1, k2 tog, k5, m1, k2 tog, k5, m2, k2 tog, k2.

Row 9: Sl 1, k3, m1, k2 tog, k1, m1, k2 tog, k4, m2, k2 tog, k5, m2, k2 tog, k1, turn.

Row 10: Sl 1, k2, m1, k2 tog, k6, m1, k2 tog, k9, m2, k2 tog, k1.

Row 11: Sl 1, k2, m1, k2 tog, k3, m1, k2 tog, k6, m2, k2 tog, k6, m2, k2 tog, k1, turn.

Row 12: Sl 1, k2, m1, k2 tog, k7, m1, k2 tog, k15.

Row 13: Cast off 2 sts, k5, m1, k2 tog, k2, m2, k2 tog, k4, m2, k2 tog, k7, m2, k2 tog, k1, turn.

Row 14: Sl 1, k2, m1, k2 tog, k8, (m1, k2 tog, k5) twice, m2, k2 tog, k2.

Rows 1–14 complete the extra rows worked at commencement of collar.

Row 15: Sl 1, k3, m1, k2 tog, k1, m1, k2 tog, k4, m2, k2 tog, k5, m2, k2 tog, k8, m2, k2 tog, k1.

Row 16: Sl 1, k2, m1, k2 tog, k9, m1, k2 tog, k6, m1, k2 tog, k9, m2, k2 tog, k1.

Row 17: Sl 1, k2, m1, k2 tog, k3, m1, k2 tog, k6, m2, k2 tog, k6, m2, k2 tog, k9, m2, k2.

Row 18: Sl 1, k2, m1, k2 tog, k10, m1, k2 tog, k7, m1, k2 tog, k15.

Row 19: Cast off 2 sts, k5, m1, k2 tog, k2, m2, k2 tog, k4, m2, k2 tog, k7, m2, k2 tog, k12.

Row 20: Cast off 10 sts, k3 (not counting st on needle after cast off), m1, k2 tog, k8, (m1, k2 tog, k5) twice, m2, k2 tog, k2.

Repeat rows 15–20 when the collar is long enough for your requirements.

End with the following rows:

Row 1: Sl 1, k3, m1, k2 tog, k1, m1, k2 tog, k4, m2, k2 tog, k5, m2, k2 tog, k8, m2, k2 tog, k1.

Row 2: Sl 1, k2, m1, k2 tog, k9, m1, k2 tog, k6, m1, k2 tog, k1, turn.

Row 3: Sl 1, k3, m2, k2 tog, k6, m2, k2 tog, k9, m2, k2.

Row 4: Sl 1, k2, m1, k2 tog, k10, m1, k2 tog, k7, m1, k2 tog, k1, turn.

Row 5: Sl 1, k3, m2, k2 tog, k7, m2, k2 tog, k12.

Row 6: Cast off 10 sts, k3, m1, k2 tog, k8, m1, k2 tog, k1, turn.

Row 7: Sl 1, k3, m2, k2 tog, k8, m2, k2 tog, k1.

Row 8: Sl 1, k2, m1, k2 tog, k9, m1, k2 tog, k1, turn.

Row 9: Sl 1, k3, m2, k2 tog, k9, m2, k2.

Row 10: Sl 1, k2, m1, k2 tog, k10, m1, k2 tog, k1, turn.

Row 11: Sl 1, k3, m2, k2 tog, k12.

Row 12: Cast off 10 sts, k3, m1, k2 tog, k1, turn.

Row 13: Sl 1, k3, m2, k2 tog, k1.

Row 14: Sl 1, k2, m1, k2 tog, k1.

Row 15: Sl 1, k3, m2, k2.

Row 16: Sl 1, k2, m1, k2 tog, k23, m2, k2 tog, k1.

Row 17: Sl 1, k2, m1, k2 tog, k27.

Cast off.

To fasten collar run a fine cord or ribbon through the small holes, draw up to fit neck and tie in bow.

ACANTHUS

Cast on 40 sts.

Row 1: K37, m1, k2 tog, k1.

Row 2: Sl 1, p to end of row.

Row 3: Cast off 28 sts, k8, m1, k2 tog, k1.

Row 4: Sl 1, k11.

Row 5: K9, m1, k2 tog, k1.

Row 6: Sl 1, k2, p9.

Row 7: K9, m1, k2 tog, k1.

Row 8: Sl 1, k11.

Row 9: K9, m1, k2 tog, k1.

Row 10: Sl 1, k2, p to end of row.

A gathering of bears wearing collars of white cotton knitting. Clockwise from lower left we have Selinarctos, Acanthus, Auricula sitting on Acanthus' knee, Albert in the bow tie (this pattern appears on page 113), Ramson in the double collar and Hellebore. The tiny bear in the front is wearing a small version of the Albert bow tie.

Row 11: K9, m1, k2 tog, k1.
Row 12: Sl 1, k11, cast on 28 sts.
Row 13: K37, m1, k2 tog, k1.
Row 14: Sl 1, k2, p to end of row.
Row 15: Cast off 28 sts, k8, m1, k2 tog, k1.
Row 16: Sl 1, k11.
Row 17: K9, m1, k2 tog, k1.
Row 18: Sl 1, k2, k9.
Row 19: K9, m1, k2 tog, k1.
Row 20: Sl 1, k10. Turn up the end of the narrow knitting and knit a st from the first cast-off sts together with the last st on the needle, thus forming a loop.
Row 21: K9, m1, k2 tog, k1.
Row 22: Sl 1, k2, p8. Again join the bar to the heading by purling a st from the cast-on sts together with the last st on the needle.
Row 23: K9, m1, k2 tog, k1.
Row 24: Sl 1, k11, cast on 28 sts.
Repeat rows 12–24 until length desired, then cast off.

AURICULA

Cast on 8 sts.
Row 1: Knit.
Row 2: Sl 1, k1, m1, p2 tog, k2, m3, k2.
Row 3: K2, (k1, p1, k1) in m3 of previous row, k2, m1, p2 tog, k2.
Row 4: Sl 1, k1, m1, p2 tog, k7.
Row 5: K7, m1, p2 tog, k2.
Row 6: Sl 1, k1, m1, p2 tog, k7.
Row 7: Cast off 3 sts, k3, m1, p2 tog, k2.
Repeat rows 2–7 until length desired.
Cast off.

RAMSON

Cast on 26 sts.
Rows 1 and 2: Knit.
Row 3: Cast off 22 sts, k to end of row.
Row 4: K4, cast on 22 sts thus: turn after knitting the 4 sts. Insert right-hand needle between first 2 sts. Draw the loop between the 2 sts and place on left hand needle. Continue increasing using the two needle method.
Rows 5 and 6: Knit.
Row 7: Cast off 2 sts, k to end.
Repeat rows 4–7 until collar is desired size.

HELLEBORE

Cast on 5 sts.
Knit 1 row.
Row 1: Sl 1, k2, m1, k2.
Row 2: Sl 1, k1, (k1, p1, k1, p1) in m1 of previous row, k3.
Rows 3 and 4: Knit.
Row 5: Sl 1, k2, (m1, k1) 6 times.
Rows 6 and 7: Knit.
Row 8: Cast off 10 sts, k4.
Repeat from row 1 for length desired; at the end of the 7th row pick up and knit the 3rd cast-off st of the previous scallop. Turn and work the 8th row casting off 11 sts, the first one being the extra st which connects the scallops. Continue until the collar is the size required. Insert ribbon through ends and tie at back, or use a button and loop fastening for a neater closure.

Bibliography

Abbey, Barbara: *Knitting Lace,* Schoolhouse Press, Pittsville, Wisconsin, reprinted 1993

De Dillmont, Thérèse: *Encyclopedia of Needlework,* DMC Publication, Mullhouse, France 1924

Fancy and Practical Knitting, 1897, The Butterick Publishing Co., London and New York

Klickman, Flora: *The Modern Knitting Book,* The Girls' Own and Woman's Magazine, London 1914

Lewis, Susanna E.: *Knitting Lace,* Taunton Press, USA 1992

Mrs Leach's Fancy Work Basket, R.S. Cartwright, London 1887

Needlecraft Practical Journals, W. Briggs & Co. Ltd, 34 Cannon Street, Manchester, *circa* 1911, 1930

Rutt, The Rt Rev Richard: *A History of Hand Knitting,* B.T. Batsford Ltd, London 1987

Sibbald and Souter, *Dainty Work for Busy Fingers,* S.W. Partridge & Co Ltd, London 1915

Thomas, Mary: *Mary Thomas's Book of Knitting Patterns,* Hodder & Stoughton Ltd, London 1985

Weldon's Practical Knitter, series, Weldon Ltd, The Strand, London *circa* 1890–1911

Wright, Mary: *Cornish Guernseys and Knit Frocks,* Alison Hodges, Cornwall 1979

Wright, Mary: *Granny's Lace Knitting* and *Great Granny's Lace Knitting,* self published, Cornwall 1986

Zimmerman, Elizabeth: *Knitter's Almanac,* Dover, New York 1981

Zimmerman, Elizabeth: *Knitting Around,* Schoolhouse Press, Pittsville, Wisconsin 1989

Guilds

The British Knitting and Crochet Guild
Membership Secretary: Anne Budsworth
228 Chester Road North
Kidderminster
Worcestershire DY10 1TH Great Britain

Handknitters Guild Inc
40 Story Street
Parkville Victoria 3052
Australia

The Knitters' Guild of NSW Inc.
The Guild Secretary
PO Box 70
Bexley South NSW 2207
Australia

Suppliers

DMC Needlecraft Pty Ltd
51-55 Carrington Road
Marrickville NSW 2204
(02) 559 3088

Fyshwick Antique Centre
77 Wollongong Street
Fyshwick ACT 2609
(06) 280 4541

Bendigo Woollen Mills
Lansell Street
Bendigo Vic 3550
(054) 42 4600

Champion Textiles
16 O'Connell Street
Newtown NSW 2042
(02) 519 6677
(Mail order service)

Queanbeyan Books and Prints
Millhouse Gallery
49 Collett Street
Queanbeyan NSW 2620
(06) 297 3067

The Sewing Spot
Shop 7, Crawford Centre
Crawford Street
Queanbeyan NSW 2620
(06) 297 1695

Kid's Scene (Susie Wilson)
Manuka Arcade
Manuka ACT 2603
(06) 239 6018

Craft Publications
Chenka Pty Ltd
83 Wollongong Street
Fyshwick ACT 2609
(06) 280 6855

Kathie Savage Studio for Dolls
  and Bears
251 Kennedys Bush Road
Halswell
Christchurch 3
New Zealand
322 8272

Evergreen Florist
Manuka Arcade
Manuka ACT 2603
(06) 239 6718

Mill Hill Books
PO Box 4
Montville Qld 4560
(074) 42 9333
*(Mail order books and fine needles
  catalogue)*

Florrie Allan Dolly Bits
PO Box 420
Kalamunda WA 6076
*(Mail order books and fine needles
  catalogue—SAE please)*

Lloyds Kia
61 McNicholl Street
Hughes ACT 2605
(06) 281 5301
*(Qualified knitting instructor, consul-
  tant and designer. Fine needles and
  yarns. Mail order—SAE please)*

INDEX